Praise for *How to Pay Your Mortgage Off in 10 Years*

At a time when Australians are worrying about the impact of interest-rate rises, this is a welcome handbook for those wanting to stop panicking and start feeling in control of their financial future. Serina's tips are practical and pragmatic, and her worked examples help put each option into perspective so readers can apply the content to suit their circumstances. Add it to your must-read list if you've got a mortgage, or really any debt you're trying to pay off.

Lacey Filipich, financial educator and award-winning author of *Money School*

Every good financial plan involves eventually repaying your home mortgage. It's easy to say but can be hard to put into practice. *How to Pay Your Mortgage Off in 10 Years* doesn't just give you the theory behind why paying your mortgage off can work – it also provides practical suggestions that you can use to take action and get started.

Michael Miller, financial planner

T0359646

HOW TO PAY YOUR MORTGAGE OFF IN 10 YEARS

(EVEN WHEN INTEREST RATES ARE GOING UP)

SERINA BIRD

MAJOR
STREET

MAJOR STREET

First published in 2023 by Major Street Publishing Pty Ltd
info@majorstreet.com.au | +61 406 151 280 | majorstreet.com.au

NATIONAL LIBRARY OF AUSTRALIA

A catalogue record for this book is available from the National Library of Australia

Printed book ISBN: 978-1-922611-79-6
Ebook ISBN: 978-1-922611-80-2

Cover design by Tess McCabe
Internal design by Production Works
Printed in Australia by Griffin Press.

10 9 8 7 6 5 4 3 2 1

Contents

PART I

TAKE A GOOD LOOK AT YOURSELF

Chapter 1

On being mortgage free

My name is Serina. I own my own home, mortgage free.

I love fashion and a bit of bling. I love to dress up for meetings, for functions and just because.

I love to travel. I take my family skiing each winter, and we enjoyed a family cruise around New Zealand last Christmas. While on our trip, we sailed into Milford Sound on Boxing Day in perfect, still weather, enjoyed a tour of art deco architecture in a vintage car at Napier, had cocktails most nights with dinner and soaked in hot springs – I even got a massage.

I love that I was able to buy my kids a gaming computer – each – with dual monitors, plus laptops and tablets. I am relieved that I'm able to afford serious orthodontic work for my eldest son. And I love being able to travel with my youngest son to attend table tennis meetups and tournaments.

My husband Neil and I don't have any money owing on our home. We live in a comfortable three-bedroom apartment in a leafy inner suburb of Canberra. We have no car loan. We pay our credit cards off in full every month. I have good superannuation – my husband has even better superannuation – and we have other investments including exchange traded funds (ETFs) and a few higher-risk angel investments. We have three investment properties.

Four years ago, I quit my job. It was a tense time in my department, and I was stressed and unhappy. Quitting when I did allowed me to spend time with my boys during the devastating bushfires (our community was blanketed in thick smoke for three months), the COVID-19 pandemic and other difficult times. It also allowed me space to explore some startup dreams, start a savings and investment podcast, write another book and do more freelance writing.

We have an enviable social life. We are blessed to have many friends, and we go out often (or often-ish). Both Neil and I are active in community-based activities and associations. We love concerts, and one of my favourite things to do is to be in the front row (or at least close).

I paid off my first property, the former family home, in 2016. That was a dream of mine, and I was so proud when I reached my goal ahead of schedule. I then bought the inner-city apartment my family now lives in. Then I met Neil, he moved in, and we bought more investment properties together while paying off the mortgage on the apartment.

It is possible.

Of course, life hasn't always been like this. My current financial situation didn't happen overnight. It took years of discipline and focus. While it's not such a big deal now if I want to splurge occasionally, for many years I was extremely frugal in my personal spending. I rarely took holidays, bought concert tickets (or went out at all) or bought new clothes. I even grew my hair long so that I could go without haircuts.

I once went to a Christmas party where a couple proudly shared that they had bought a new car. Another was going on an overseas trip. Those luxuries simply weren't on my radar at that time, but my frugal approach was more than worth it. I gained momentum on investing and paying down my mortgage, and I reached my goal even faster than I had planned. Now my husband and I jointly work towards building our wealth, and that period of frugality set us up well for our future investing discipline. From little habits, big things grow.

No-one said it would be easy

You may have heard of the marshmallow experiment. It's one of the most famous studies about delayed gratification, conducted by psychologist Walter Mischel and his colleagues at Stanford University in the late 1960s and early 1970s. In the experiment, young children were taken to a room where there was one marshmallow on a table. They were told they could either eat the marshmallow right away or they could wait a few minutes and receive a second one.

Could you resist the temptation to eat a marshmallow if you knew it would be doubled in a few minutes' time? Some children could, but many couldn't. The significance of the experiment is that the study found the children able to delay gratification tended to have higher academic achievement, better social skills and other positive life outcomes. I would expect that they would also tend to be better investors.

How much are you currently paying in rent, or on your mortgage repayments? Can you change aspects of your current lifestyle now to reduce your home loan debt and pay your mortgage off earlier? Even within 10 years? Even when interest rates go up for a period of the term of the loan?

If you can, it stands to reason that a few years down the track you'll have more money for marshmallows, figuratively speaking. With your mortgage a thing of the past, the money you had been spending on repayments will suddenly be free for other things. That sounds pretty good, doesn't it? I guess that's why you're reading this book!

Home ownership is never easy

Before we go any further, I want to talk about the affordability of home ownership and how it has affected different generations. While it won't help you pay your mortgage faster, it will help to explain why your mortgage is so large and put today's struggles into the larger context.

I was having coffee with a finance writer last year when I mentioned, in passing, one of my investment properties and some issues I was dealing with. The mood turned icy. I could see the (younger) guy was struggling with an inner rage.

'Oh, shit,' I thought to myself. 'He thinks I'm an entitled gen-X property owner. This could get ugly.'

And yes, he had some awful stories. As we talked, I learned that his experience had been of greedy landlords who overcharge, fail to undertake essential maintenance and abuse their position of privilege. He, and many in his generation, felt that the high cost of housing had pushed home ownership out of his reach – and that the generations before, especially those who are now property investors, are to blame.

He's probably sick of being told he just needs to tighten his belt, cut back on lattes and ditch the avocado toast – especially when other generations are free to indulge. From his perspective, the difficulty in reaching home ownership can't be solved just by forgoing a few little luxuries, like occasional brunch.

He does have a point. Research *does* show that overall the path to home ownership is harder than ever before – especially due to the high cost of housing. According to Dr Peter Tulip, chief economist at the Centre for Independent Studies, 'home owners, or households, as a group are paying a larger share of their income in interest than they did in the 1980s'. As interest rates go up, the sheer size of many mortgages is putting unprecedented stress on household budgets.

I don't need to be an economist to see that housing affordability is an issue: all I have to do is start searching for property online or talk to first home buyers about their mortgages. Cost of living is a hot political issue, especially as it's becoming more and more expensive to buy a dream home.

I was lucky that I bought my first home – the former family home – on the upswing of a major property boom in early 2001. My former husband and I then started investing in property around 2004. We had some more luck catching a Canberra property mini-boom and continued building our portfolio over the next nine years. But that's when the luck ended.

It all came unstuck when I filed for a Domestic Violence Order in the ACT Magistrates Court in August 2014 – and again the next year. Suddenly, I was a single mother with two young kids to support. While I had a good job, I was battling the highest childcare costs in Australia, legal bills and 10 negatively geared mortgages. At the same time, the rental income from those investment properties plummeted, in some cases by 40 per cent.

I could have lost everything, but I didn't. While my department at work wasn't exactly compassionate, my job was at least stable. I communicated regularly with the bank. In the process of separation, my ex-husband and I sold off properties: one sold to a developer at a larger than expected profit, others brought more moderate returns and one sold for a loss. This freed up equity and meant we could reduce debt.

My big lesson from all of this was the importance of not over-extending yourself and ensuring you have sufficient reserves for the unexpected. The Royal Commission into Misconduct in the Banking, Superannuation and Financial Services Industry unearthed stories of over-geared property investors, just like me, who *did* lose everything when the unexpected happened. Looking back, though we thought we were doing the smart thing by buying properties, renting them out and investing in shares and index funds, I'm not sure we got better returns than we would have had we just knuckled down, paid off our mortgage on our home and contributed more to our superannuation. It certainly would have been less stressful.

I'm sharing my experience because it's easy for first home owners and those just getting started to assume that everyone in previous generations had a smooth ride – especially when mortgages are hitting record highs, wages aren't keeping up with inflation and interest rates are continuing to rise. However, it's important to remember that everyone has their own story, and everyone has faced their own challenges.

Going through separation and the resulting money stress was challenging, but I'm resilient, and it made me a stronger person. I'm very grateful that I made it through with solid property assets. I remember joking to my family lawyer that it could have been worse: as at least there was money to lose. She became serious in response and told me that one of her other clients was going through personal insolvency. Yes, it happens to many people who go through relationship breakdowns.

Looking beyond my personal story and experiences now, there is the sad fact that women in their late 50s have the fastest growing rate of homelessness in the country. Homelessness and housing stress in Canberra, where I live, is made more acute by some of Australia's highest rents. For some older Australians, elder abuse is also a problem, and we know that the elderly are at heightened risk of financial scams.

Positive difference for today's buyers

This is not a book that is intended to make you feel bad for enjoying life. I have many hacks for saving money, and it's up to you whether and how you choose to implement them. I will not judge you or your financial priorities. Nor am I going to suggest that paying your mortgage off early will be easy; for many people it will require focus, discipline and strategy. However, I *am* going to tell you that it *can* be done – and I'm going to give you strategies and motivation to help you do it.

Although home ownership is less affordable than ever before – you're not imagining it! – engaging in intergenerational warfare is not productive. Cher may have hoped to turn back time, but it just isn't possible. And being consumed by a 'what about me – it isn't fair' attitude doesn't help to pay down your mortgage. Every generation has its challenges but also its own unique opportunities, so I want to finish this chapter by examining some of the *advantages* of being or becoming a home owner today.

Less bias in obtaining a loan

Once upon a time, a bank manager (usually a white, middle-aged man) would decide who qualified for a home loan – and who didn't. You had to make an appointment for an in-person interview with that person. Unsurprisingly, most successful applicants were also white men. Diversity wasn't really a thing – and that wasn't so long ago. Ita Buttrose, ABC Chair at the time of writing, founding editor of *Cleo* and the former editor of *The Australian Women's Weekly*, was a young and powerful woman in the media in the 1970s and 1980s, but even as a working mum of two she struggled to get a loan on her own.

Now, more women are buying property than ever before. In fact, in 2022 the number of single women who bought a home almost matched that of single men. That correlates with my observation that young women are increasingly buying their first home before they meet and settle down with a partner.

Australia is also a much more multicultural community than it used to be. While bias and barriers do still exist, being able to apply for loans digitally rather than having to be interviewed in person at the bank branch by a white, middle-class, middle-aged man should make it easier for people from culturally and linguistically diverse communities to obtain mortgages.

Access to digital banking

I remember getting my first full-time job and having to run out to the bank at lunchtime to deposit a cheque for rental payments. These days, all those sorts of payments can be made online. Not only that, you can automate your loan repayments. (This is usually set up soon after you receive your mortgage funds.) You can even automate additional payments and make one-off payments whenever you like. For instance, if you decide not to buy something, you could transfer that amount straight onto your mortgage. We'll discuss mortgage repayment strategies later in this book.

More flexible working arrangements

There are now more and more opportunities to work from home, which can mean a fortune in saved travel costs (more on this in chapter 9). It can also mean that you can practise geographical arbitrage – basically, you can earn a city salary while living in a cheaper area, perhaps even one more suited to your lifestyle ambitions, such as a small country town.

For example, Misty and her husband wanted to buy a home for themselves, their two boys and their golden retriever Terry. But with Canberra experiencing a property boom that suddenly made it the most expensive city in Australia in which to rent, making their home ownership dreams difficult to realise, they decided to do things differently. They bought a four-bedroom home in Chinchilla, around three hours west of Brisbane, for $250,000 – less than a quarter of the price they would have paid in Canberra. Misty's husband was able to convince his department to allow him to work remotely, and the family quickly made friends in their new community. 'It's like winning lotto,' Misty often says of their tree change.

Availability of online comparison tools

The internet has revolutionised our capacity to research, and this includes the ability to compare the best possible interest rate for our mortgages using online comparison tools. Don't forget to check out the fees as well, as they will impact the overall cost of your loan. Good sources for this information include *Money* (specifically its annual 'Best of the Best' awards), Canstar, Finder and InfoChoice.

You could even ask Siri or Alexa if you don't want to type everything into a search engine, and behavioural retargeting means that once you start searching you're likely to be advertised mortgage deals for weeks. (Just be sure to do your research before choosing one of those options.) Simply put, there is no excuse in this day and age for *not* spending a bit of time informing yourself about the best mortgage rate.

Convenience of side hustles

It is now easier than ever to pick up a side hustle and earn extra income to pay off your mortgage faster. Whether it's listing your services on Airtasker, selling crafts on Etsy or doing some freelance writing, the opportunities supported and made convenient by today's technology are astounding. These side hustles can even grow to become large and profitable businesses. We'll discuss generating additional income in greater detail in chapter 13.

Greater competition in the market

In the 'old days', it was generally only the major banks or credit unions that offered mortgages. Recently, many new non-bank lenders have emerged that offer mortgages, such as Firstmac, loans.com.au and Pepper Money. There are also divisions of major banks that offer internet-based loan services, such as UBank (NAB) and Unloan (CommBank). These lenders don't even have a storefront, and you usually apply for loans online. Because they are not heavily invested in physical assets such as real estate in expensive CBD locations, they can usually pass on competitive rates to borrowers. The greatest advantage of these new players in the market, however, is that more competition between lenders for borrowers results in better deals. Exploit that!

Power of dual incomes

It wasn't that long ago that most households got by on a single income. For instance, until 1966 female Commonwealth public servants were required to resign upon marriage. These days it's the norm for women to work, and most households are on a dual income. Notwithstanding the persistent gender pay gap and the high cost of childcare, many families now have more than one person earning an income. This means it's possible to work together to pay off a home sooner.

Summary

- If you don't have a mortgage or rent to pay every month, you have more income to do other things – whether that's travelling, pursuing a passion or not working at all.

- People who practise delayed gratification (that's waiting before splurging) are more likely to be successful in life. Pausing on discretionary spending now to pay off your mortgage will let you reap huge rewards in the future.

- Home owners are currently paying a larger share of their income in mortgage repayments than they did previously – and this will increase as interest rates get higher.
- Buying a home and paying off a mortgage are more difficult than ever before, but life in the 2020s still offers many advantages to help you achieve your home ownership goals.

Now that I've painted a picture of what life without a mortgage on your home can look like, shared my own story (the good and the bad) and discussed both the challenges and the advantages of achieving home ownership today, it's time to crunch some numbers. In the next chapter we're going to explore why paying your mortgage off – and quickly – is a sound financial strategy.

Chapter 2

Crunching the numbers

$601,797

That's the size of the average mortgage for owner-occupied dwellings in November 2022 according to the Australian Bureau of Statistics (ABS). Not only is this large – more than half a million dollars – but it has also grown 36 per cent since 2018.

This is daunting. For many people, paying their mortgage off feels impossible – or worse. In a February 2023 *ABC News* article, Sally Tindall from Rate City described the feeling of having a mortgage as 'like a life sentence', especially for young first home buyers.

In this book, I'm going to show a stack of tips and tricks that can help you to ditch your mortgage in just 10 years. It won't be a walk in the park, and not everything I suggest will be right for you and your personal circumstances. Still, if you make being mortgage free your priority and start taking action right now, you might be surprised how quickly you reach your goal.

Let's start with the loan

For ease and simplicity, I'm going to round down the cost of the average mortgage to $600,000. Averages hide detail, and your loan is unlikely to reflect the average precisely. You may have borrowed more, or perhaps you borrowed less. No matter how much you borrowed, many of the principles are the same.

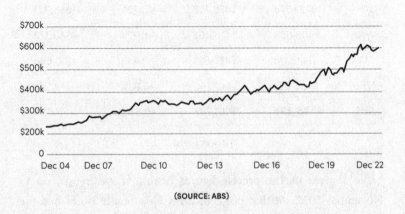

Figure 1: Average loan sizes for owner–occupier dwellings across Australia

(SOURCE: ABS)

The size of the average loan also varies according to where you live. As you can see in figure 1, overall loan sizes rose dramatically in the 18 years to December 2022. What this figure doesn't show is that the average mortgage in New South Wales sits well above the nation-wide average, peaking at $803,235 in January 2022.

The property market has come off the boil a little since then. Interest rates have started rising, fewer properties are selling and banks are (for the first time in years) scrambling to get new customers. This is great news for those seeking to negotiate a good deal (more on that in chapter 5).

Table 1: Average loan size by state and territory

	November 2021	November 2022	Annual change (%)	Annual change ($)
NSW	$769,701	$752,164	-2.28%	-$17,537
ACT	$596,105	$636,749	+6.82%	+$40,644
VIC	$619,844	$618,109	-0.28%	-$1,735
QLD	$512,771	$532,535	+3.85%	+$19,764
SA	$423,276	$479,253	+13.22%	+$55,977
WA	$438,084	$478,462	+9.22%	+$40,378
TAS	$448,118	$459,016	+2.43%	+$10,898
NT	$436,223	$440,260	+0.93%	+4,037
AUS	**$595,898**	**$601,797**	**+0.99%**	**+$5,899**

(SOURCE: ABS)

Table 1 gives us the precise figures behind those trends, up to November 2022. At that point in time, New South Wales had the highest average loan size at $752,164, which was actually an annual decrease of 2.28 per cent. ACT, where I live, came in second at $636,749, which is above the national average of $601,797. This figure took me by surprise, as property prices were low when I moved to the territory a couple of decades ago, with many (non-Canberrans) turning up their noses at moving to the nation's capital. (Canberra also currently has the nation's highest rents.) Third on the list is Victoria, with an average loan size of $618,109. Even Tasmania, a place where tree changers traditionally moved in search of cheap(er) property, carries an average loan size of $459,016, which was an annual increase of 2.43 per cent.

It seems like mortgages are large in many parts of Australia.

And now the repayments

Having a large mortgage is one thing. Servicing it is another.

A few years ago, interest rates were at record low levels – one of the factors that led to the boom in housing from 2020 to 2022. While I didn't buy in that market, I know many who did; it was a crazy time, and FOMO (fear of missing out) was in full force.

You may be one of those who bought a home for the first time in that period. Back then, there was talk of interest rates being low for years, with Reserve Bank of Australia Governor Philip Lowe publicly saying that interest rates would not rise until at least 2024. Some people were speculating that interest rates may even go as low as zero. However, the Reserve Bank has since gone against its earlier indications, lifting interest rates ten times consecutively between May 2022 and March 2023, and taking the benchmark rate from 0.1 per cent to 3.6 per cent.

The Australian economy recorded record inflation rates of 7.8 per cent in January 2023, driven by factors such as supply chain shortages, the higher price of petrol (affecting transportation) and the impact of the floods on food production. This is the highest rate of inflation Australia has experienced since 1990. According to Lowe, inflation needs to come down to within a 2 to 3 per cent range, and the Reserve Bank will lift interest rates to dampen spending accordingly. Lowe describes inflation as 'corrosive' and warns that it puts pressure on household budgets, erodes savings, increases inequality and hurts those on low incomes.

What frightens people are memories of when the official Reserve Bank cash rate peaked at 17.5 per cent in January 1990, when many families lost their homes due to crippling interest-rate repayments. At the time of writing, there is no indication that interest rates will go that high, but it has people panicking and worrying – especially with the large size of mortgages.

Even an increase of the official cash rate to 3.5 per cent has marked a significant increase in what many people thought they would be paying for their home. Add to this the cost of living pressures, including higher petrol and food expenses. One of the COVID trends was people moving away from congested inner-city environments out to the suburbs. At the time, petrol was cheap and many people were working from home, so transport wasn't an issue. But now, for many of us, it is.

It's not just recent home buyers who have been affected. Many people fixed their interest rates to take advantage of historically low rates (more on fixed loans versus variable loans in chapter 5). In 2023, around 800,000 people have come off or are coming off those fixed rates and into a higher interest-rate environment (and I, for my investment loans, am one of them).

Ouch.

Lenders *should* have considered serviceability at a higher level when approving loans during low-interest-rate boom times. Still, for many borrowers, knowing they will have to pay more if conditions change and then actually finding themselves liable for the increased interest payments are two very different things.

According to the National Australia Bank (NAB), around 75 per cent of Australians live from payday to payday. That leaves them exposed to big interest-rate rises. And selling a property bought in recent years because making the repayments has become difficult might not be a viable option for some due to the falling market. By the time fees and commissions are considered, there might not be much money left. Some properties may even sell at a loss.

So, how much has the cost of a mortgage gone up? Table 2 sets out monthly repayments at a range of rates on a $600,000 loan, assuming zero account-keeping and other fees, a 30-year loan term, and a principal-and-interest structure.

Table 2: Monthly repayments on a $600,000 loan

Rate	Monthly repayments	Estimated total interest
3.50% p.a.	$2694	$369,937
4.00% p.a.	$2864	$431,217
4.50% p.a.	$3040	$494,440
5.00% p.a.	$3221	$559,535
5.50% p.a.	$3407	$626,424
6.00% p.a.	$3597	$695,029
6.50% p.a.	$3792	$765,267
7.00% p.a.	$3992	$837,053
7.50% p.a.	$4195	$910,303
8.00% p.a.	$4403	$984,931

(CALCULATIONS COMPLETED AT MONEYSMART.GOV.AU)

When you look at this table, you can see a clear trend. Obviously, the higher the interest rate, the higher the repayment. Many mortgage holders have been shocked by the steep increase in repayments due to increasing interest rates.

It's important to also look at the amount of interest that is payable over the life of the loan. The higher the interest rate, the greater the compounding effect. In other words, you are going to pay a lot more interest overall – in many cases, more than the cost of the original mortgage over the life of the loan. Of course, property values usually go up (especially over 30 years), but they don't always.

Note that these repayments are for a 30-year loan term. To repay in 10 years, you need to make higher repayments. If you've ever had a credit card and only paid the minimum, you'll have experienced the compounding effect. I'll talk about compound interest and how much you will need to pay – and why it's important to break down the principal – in the next chapter. For now, table 2 is useful as a snapshot of how much it costs just to tread water.

Why pay off your mortgage quickly?

When you first get a mortgage, it is usually set for around 30 years. Many borrowers are happy to sit and take that long to pay it off. It can also take even longer than that, with some people choosing to refinance or withdraw equity from their loans to pay for things such as holidays, cars and renovations. You might think this is crazy, but it can make sense to pay for your car loan from your mortgage as interest is charged at a lower rate than a car loan – provided you increase your repayments to compensate. Withdrawing money from your home to pay for lifestyle issues is something else entirely. Still, many people do it.

There will also be readers of this book who follow many of the strategies I outline but decide for one reason or another to keep a small mortgage. Some will find the discipline required to pay off their mortgage in 10 years too hard to maintain. Others will encounter unforeseen hurdles (and we cover what to do in these cases throughout this book). But getting ahead in your repayments and increasing your equity, even in some small way, will help you reach many of the following positive outcomes.

I want to recognise that not everyone is fortunate enough to be able to buy – or pay off – a home. As I write, Australia is experiencing an acute housing shortage with skyrocketing rents and a lack of social housing. One of my friends contacted me recently for advice on finding a rental property urgently as she and her two children needed to move. Thankfully, they found a stopgap solution, but this is a real problem that many people around the country are facing.

I believe that this housing crisis is going to lead to more and more people choosing to own their own home – and pay it off quickly – to ensure they always have somewhere to live.

If you aren't a home owner yet, plenty of the budgeting, saving and money management information in this book will be helpful for your cash flow right now. If you choose to make home ownership your goal, then these tips will assist you in saving for a deposit sooner.

Achieve financial stability

As a mum with two kids – and a one-time single mum – the security of owning my own home is important to me. I want to own my own home outright and never have to worry about losing the roof over my family's heads. I believe there is something powerful about wanting to provide for my family – to build a nest, if you will. Whether we end up living in the same place all our lives or not, my desire to provide a safe and secure environment for my kids and myself is a driving force.

In Australia, our freehold system of land title means that, in effect, the government owns the land and we sort of rent it. In most places, you receive freehold title when you purchase property, and mostly it's yours. In the ACT, where I live, we don't have freehold title, so we usually purchase a 100-year lease. The reason I mention this is that sometimes, similar to what happens in the movie *The Castle*, the government wants to make a compulsory acquisition of your property. This does occasionally happen, especially for major infrastructure projects such as roads and airports, but for most home owners it isn't a risk.

Save on interest

The sooner you pay off your mortgage, the more interest you can save. How much? I'll talk more about compound interest and how it works in the next chapter, but for now let's look at the average

$600,000 mortgage and crunch some numbers based on a loan at 6 per cent.

As shown in figure 2, over the course of a 30-year mortgage you would spend $695,029 in interest payments for a $600,000 loan. That's more than the cost of the original mortgage in interest payments alone. In contrast, if you increase payments to repay the loan in 10 years, you would only pay $199,348 in interest – a saving of $495,681. That's a huge difference in both time and money.

Figure 2: Total repayments over the life of a 30-year mortgage and a 10-year mortgage

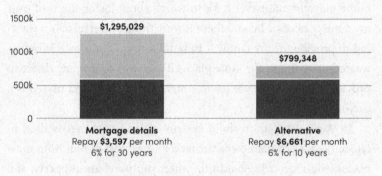

(CALCULATIONS COMPLETED AT MONEYSMART.GOV.AU)

Be prepared for emergencies

Unexpected things happen all the time: urgent car repairs, fines, you need a new oven or you even experience sudden unemployment due to a pandemic or economic downturn – who would have thought?

When I work with clients, I often ask them what they would do if they suddenly needed to find $2000 to pay for something. Their answers are enlightening and tell me whether they are prepared for the unexpected. Often, people don't have any spare cash to pay for things that aren't budgeted for. One person told me how she had recently struggled to pay for unexpected dental work – and she was in a stable, above-average-earning public service job! As I mentioned earlier, around 75 per cent of people in Australia live from payday to payday. So, when something unexpected happens, they have to resort to desperate measures, such as taking out high-interest payday loans or racking up even more credit card debt (often at around 20 per cent interest per annum).

One way to avoid this is to have an emergency fund with savings that you can dip into if needed. Expert opinion differs about the amount you require, and it really depends on your appetite for risk. Some experts suggest up to six months of income, and others say two months' worth of expenses. I generally suggest people aim for around three months' worth of income. Work out what that looks like in terms of a number, then see if that number resonates for you. For instance, if you earn $2500 a fortnight, aim to save $15,000 as an emergency fund. If you don't feel emotionally safe with this amount, add more. If you feel this is fine, you could even consider a lower amount.

The problem with most emergency funds is that often they will sit in a low-interest account, so your money isn't working hard for you. A good way to get around this is to treat your mortgage like an emergency fund by making additional repayments, knowing that you can withdraw if needed (at the bank's discretion) if you have a redraw facility.

Reduce your tax bill

If you put your money into a bank account, you will earn interest on your deposit. Those earnings will be taxed. The same happens if you receive share dividends. And if you sell your shares or other investments, you will need to pay capital gains tax. But guess what? If you are paying off your home and it's your principal place of residence, you probably won't be levied with capital gains tax if you sell (so long as you live there for over twelve months). That makes taking out a mortgage and paying it off early a tax-effective strategy. The equity you build in your home (in other words, the dollars you are ahead of your repayments, which you can often access if you have a redraw facility) aren't taxable either. That equity also reduces interest costs, so it's really a win-win.

Invest in a low-risk way

We tend to think of investing as being about going out and finding new things to invest in, but paying off debt can also be a form of investing – and it's low risk.

Consider this: you are approached to invest in a 'sure thing' scheme with a guaranteed return of 6 per cent per annum. That sounds pretty good, but that 6 per cent isn't everything. There may also be fees for applying for the investment (for example, stamp duty or loan application fees). Then there are taxes, as we covered just before. Your rate of return would look something like this:

$$(investment \times 6\%) - (investment\ costs \times 50\%\ capital\ gains\ tax) = y$$
$$y \times tax\ rate = projected\ return$$

Plus, there is the risk of the 'sure thing' investment not panning out. Meanwhile, if the interest on your mortgage is at 6 per cent, paying it off gives you an almost guaranteed return, the value of which will largely depend on how long you keep the property.

I have established that paying off your mortgage is a low-risk strategy, but there is one key risk. By adopting this conservative strategy, you risk overlooking other higher-performing investments. You could, for instance, risk missing the tax advantages of making additional contributions to your superannuation or investing in a rising share market. Certainly, it's important to contribute regularly to superannuation and invest in a range of assets, but focusing on repaying your mortgage – especially in the short term – is important as it reduces your debt and builds a solid foundation for your financial future. Furthermore, once you have a decent amount of equity (and also an emergency fund) you'll be in a better financial situation to make some (researched) higher-risk, higher-return investments. As a well-known angel investor said to me, 'Always pay off your home loan first.'

Reduce financial housing stress

Financial housing stress generally occurs when a household is spending more than one third of its gross (before tax) income on housing. It's not a hard and fast rule, and high-income earners are affected differently to more vulnerable low-income earners. Still, it's worth noting that 11.5 per cent of Australian households spent 30 to 50 per cent of their gross income on housing from 2017 to 2018, meaning many households were experiencing housing stress.

The problem with financial housing stress is that if you spend so much money on housing, you don't have much left over for other things – food, transport or education, for instance. This can perpetuate the poverty cycle. In addition, according to the Australian Institute of Health and Welfare, access to quality, affordable housing is fundamental to wellbeing. Obviously, it's ideal not to have a big mortgage in the first place, but the high cost of housing means there are limited choices. Having a strategy to smash your mortgage – and early – can be hard in the short term, but it can help to reduce your susceptibility to housing stress in the long term.

Summary

- The average size of a mortgage in Australia has grown 36 per cent since 2018, and as of November 2022 it amounted to $601,797. I use $600,000 for the calculations in this book for ease of reference.

- The monthly repayment on a $600,000 loan (assuming 6 per cent interest rate and zero fees) is $3597. Based on these assumptions, home owners will end up paying over twice their original loan in interest alone if they repay their mortgage over the typical 30-year period.
- There are several reasons to pay off your mortgage quickly, including feelings of stability, minimising the total interest paid, 'saving' money without paying tax, using it as a low-risk investment strategy and reducing long-term financial housing stress.

I've walked you through why it's a good idea to pay your mortgage off quickly, but it's worth digging a little deeper into one of those reasons in particular: saving on interest. It all comes down to some mathematical magic called 'compound interest', and in the next chapter I'm going to show you how it works and what it means for your home loan.

Chapter 3

Compound interest and your mortgage

Albert Einstein is believed to have said that compound interest is the eighth wonder of the world: 'He who understands it, earns it; he who doesn't, pays it.' While we can't be sure Einstein said those very words, it's clear that compound interest is mathematical magic – especially when it comes to home loans. Understood and used well, it can make you a millionaire. Disrespected, it can do the opposite.

Though it can be tricky, we don't have to be nuclear physicists or maths geniuses to work out how compound interest affects us. These days we have nifty online financial calculators, including the free government-supported calculator at moneysmart.gov.au, to help us out. Before we start crunching the numbers, however, let's take a step back and take a look at the history of compound interest, starting with the game of chess and some grains of rice.

The history of compound interest

There is a legend about a bargain struck between the inventor of chess and a king. Presented with the game, the king was so pleased that he offered to reward its inventor.

'Name your reward,' he said.

The inventor of chess responded, 'I only ask that you give me one grain of rice for the first square of the chessboard and that you double it for each succeeding square.'

Thinking he had gotten off lightly, the king agreed to this arrangement. He had only been asked for a few grains of rice – not gold or precious stones! Little did he realise he had made a promise that he would be unable to fulfil.

This is what the bargain looks like for the first 14 squares of the chessboard:

Square 1	1 grain
Square 2	2 grains
Square 3	4 grains
Square 4	8 grains
Square 5	16 grains
Square 6	32 grains
Square 7	64 grains
Square 8	128 grains
Square 9	256 grains
Square 10	512 grains
Square 11	1024 grains
Square 12	2048 grains
Square 13	4096 grains
Square 14	8192 grains

Notice how small this starts off – the difference of a few grains, and then just a handful of rice. But can you guess the reward owed to the inventor as the number of grains compounded across all 64 squares? Over 18 quintillion grains of rice – more than 450 billion tonnes.

Hopefully your mortgage won't double and double again (and again) in value; however, in illustrating how quickly things can grow under the compounding effect, this legend bears real relevance to today's borrowers.

Our modern financial system is based on the concept of compound interest – that is, interest compounds on interest, meaning we repay more than just the principal. The first written evidence of compound interest dates back to 2400 BCE in modern-day Iraq, but it wasn't until the 17th century that it was widely adopted in Europe.

The introduction of compound interest was revolutionary. It enabled the financial system to make a profit on lending, which made lending a business. The ready access to capital we see today as a result of this means that people can borrow money for all sorts of purposes, including running (or growing) a business and buying property. Using the same concept, the financial system pays to borrow money too, which is why you can receive interest on your bank deposits.

You might not feel like your mortgage is a blessing, but in a sense it is. Imagine if you had to wait and save up for the entire value of your home before buying. It might take a lifetime. Or, in a rising property market, you might never be able to afford to buy a home at all. You might even have to resort to an unregulated market, borrowing funds from dodgy people you would then be indebted to.

Why $1 can be more than $1

$1 = $1, right? You would think so, but it depends largely on how you earned that money, and then also on what you do with it.

A dollar earned usually has a cost. Assuming you don't work from home, think about how much it costs to drive or take the bus to work. Add up those essential pick-me-up coffees, special office outfits, contributions to farewell gifts, TGIF after-work drinks and bought lunches. And taxes – don't forget that you could pay up to 45 per cent tax on your earnings.

If you do work from home, you will likely have to pay for things such as electricity, internet and equipment. Even taking into consideration what you can claim as deductions on your tax return, there are still some costs related to working from home.

Then, once you have money in your pocket, what do you do? You could spend it. Then it would be gone. Later, knowing that you have some money coming in, you could buy something on your credit card – and a lot of people do that, particularly for job-related things such as those we've already mentioned.

This is how it plays out. Say you pay $1000 for a new suit. Looking good at work is an investment, right? Well, sort of. Looking professional at work is important, and sadly many of us are judged on what we wear. Let's now examine how this investment stacks up if you purchase it using a credit card, factoring in compound interest.

Assuming interest of 20 per cent per annum, if you paid nothing at all on your credit card balance you would owe $1200 for that suit after 12 months. What if you made the minimum repayments? Say you paid your loan back at $25 a month. Wouldn't it all be paid off fairly quickly? You would assume that as 1000 divided by 25 is 40, you would easily repay this in just over three years – but not so. If you only paid $25 a month, it would take you five years and seven months to pay off your initial $1000 plus $662 in accrued interest. All up, that sharp-looking suit you bought would cost you $1662. I'm also guessing it might not look quite as good five years later (unless you bought something really classic).

Let's consider another option now. If you doubled the amount you repaid to $50 a month, you would reduce the time it would take to pay off the suit by more than half, repaying the debt in two years and one month. You would also pay $227 in interest, which is less than a third of what you would have paid at $25 a month – just by making additional payments.

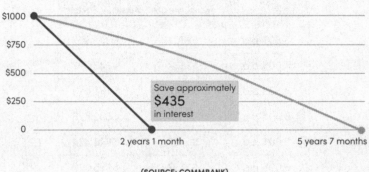

Figure 3: Comparing savings between paying $25 and $50 a month

(SOURCE: COMMBANK)

I generated figure 3 to illustrate the difference in these two approaches using CommBank's online credit card repayment calculator. If you are carrying credit card debt, jump online, enter the details of your debt and see how much you can save by paying off just a little more at a time. Of course, if you can pay your credit card off in full within the interest-free period, you will pay *nothing* in interest. Did you know that, depending on your credit card, you can get up to 55 days interest-free on purchases? (As I will discuss in chapter 5, using a credit card can be a good strategy for blitzing your mortgage – but only if you know you have the discipline to manage it responsibly.) Additionally, if you save up and pay in cash (or from a debit card) you'll save even more because you won't have to pay annual card fees (or merchant fees, which are often charged at the point of sale).

Compound interest and the size of your mortgage

In chapter 2 I looked at the size of repayments on a $600,000 mortgage at different interest rates, showing how repayments increase as the interest rate goes up. Let's look at those figures again in table 3.

Table 3: Monthly repayments on a $600,000 loan

Rate	Monthly repayments	Estimated total interest
3.50% p.a.	$2694	$369,937
4.00% p.a.	$2864	$431,217
4.50% p.a.	$3040	$494,440
5.00% p.a.	$3221	$559,535
5.50% p.a.	$3407	$626,424
6.00% p.a.	$3597	$695,029
6.50% p.a.	$3792	$765,267
7.00% p.a.	$3992	$837,053
7.50% p.a.	$4195	$910,303
8.00% p.a.	$4403	$984,931

The higher the interest rate, the higher the rate of compounding. This means that getting the lowest possible interest rate matters; it's one of the best ways of achieving the goal of paying off a mortgage in 10 years. (Of course, interest rates are broadly out of our control – more on high- and low-interest environments in a moment – but I do have some tips for snagging the best deals in the next chapter.)

Knowing what we do about the compounding effect and assuming an interest rate of 6 per cent, to pay off a mortgage of $600,000 in 10 years – rather than the typical 30 years assumed in table 3 – you would need to pay $6661 a month. That's almost double the monthly payments the bank recommends you make on a 30-year term. If interest rates went up to 7 per cent, you would need to pay $6967 a month to pay off that same mortgage in 10 years.

These numbers may seem incredible. Daunting. Unrealistic. Crazy. But here's the thing: even small amounts repaid early will have a dramatic impact on your mortgage, reducing both the time it takes to pay it off in full and the amount of interest you will pay over the life of the loan.

Let's go back to that $1; $1 paid on your mortgage in year one of a 30-year mortgage does not equal $1. Assuming an interest rate of 6 per cent, that $1 is the equivalent to $1.06 *in the first year*. In other words, it 'saved' you having to pay 6 cents in interest over the course of that single year. That might not sound like much, but remember that you're likely to pay off more than a single additional dollar at a time – and that next year your savings will compound. Just like with the credit card example I gave earlier in this chapter, compound interest in practice means that the principal is increasing if you don't pay it down quickly.

It is difficult to calculate the exact impact that small, one-off amounts have on your mortgage because there are so many variables. However, while the total compounded value of paying $1 off is hard to show, I can tell you that the true value of paying $1 off your mortgage is somewhere between $1.78 and $6. I can also show you that even small amounts, paid regularly, can make a huge difference to the term of your loan and the total interest saved. For instance, say you pay an extra $100 a month on a typical $600,000 mortgage at 6 per cent with zero fees. For most people, $100 in savings isn't hard to find over the course of a month, especially using my tips in part II. That's equivalent to $25 a week, which you might even be able to save by reducing your intake of barista-made coffee. (Yes, you can still enjoy coffee – the key word here is *reducing*.) That extra $100 each month would enable you to own your home in 27 years and 11 months – two years and one month ahead of the typical 30 years. It would also enable you to save $58,265 in interest payments. If you make additional repayments of $100 a fortnight you will own your home in 24 years and four months, and save $154,779 in interest. (I cover why fortnightly payments help in chapter 5.)

Compound interest can be complicated to calculate, particularly if maths isn't really your thing, and that's why online mortgage calculators are revolutionary. As with calculating debt repayments on your credit card (mentioned earlier), you can enter in the balance of your mortgage, your repayments and your interest rate, and you will be able to quickly calculate how variables such as additional repayments and changes in interest rates can affect your bottom line. I always do this when setting a mortgage repayment goal, and I find it motivating (more on goal-setting and mindset in the next chapter). It can be almost addictive, seeing the impact that paying back more on your mortgage can have. Good online calculators can be found on most banks' or financial institutions' websites, at moneysmart.gov.au and at finance author Noel Whittaker's website.

Before you even ask, yes, banks and financial institutions do occasionally get their compound interest calculations wrong. If maths *is* your thing, you might want to run your eye over your statements from time to time.

Even if you are not able to double your mortgage repayments and blitz your mortgage in 10 years, if you make regular additional repayments you will own your home sooner and save on interest payments.

High- and low-interest-rate environments

When interest rates are high, it can feel as if you're not getting ahead on your mortgage – and that's due to the compounding effect.

Even if you're paying more per month in your regular repayments, it can look like you aren't making much of a dent in your principal because a larger chunk of your repayments is for interest.

On the other hand, in a high-interest-rate environment you are likely to get as high a rate of return from paying off your mortgage as you would on other investments (or higher). Even if the interest rate on your mortgage is 10 per cent, how many other investments can offer a guaranteed, tax-free return that beats it? Not many.

It's not just mortgage rates that go up, either. The interest on bank deposits and yields on other loan-type investments such as bonds will (usually) go up as well. Consequently, the share market (in general) tends to do less well in high-interest-rate environments, with many people choosing to pay down debt or invest.

Conversely, in low-interest-rate environments the best strategy is likely to be different. Investors typically won't park their money in low-interest bank accounts or purchase low-interest-yielding bonds. When interest rates are low, they can often get a better yield just on dividends alone. This can (in general) lead to an upswing in the share market. Accordingly, in low-interest-rate environments, you can often get a better rate of return elsewhere than you would paying off your mortgage.

However, I'm a firm believer that whatever the interest-rate environment, it's important to prioritise making additional repayments on your mortgage. Regardless of whether you can get higher returns elsewhere, paying down your mortgage tends to be a lower-risk option. I believe that it's often a fundamentally good idea to decrease your overall risk by first reducing your debts, as explored earlier in this chapter, before considering investing elsewhere. That said, this does depend on your appetite for risk.

To my mind, prioritising paying your mortgage in a low-interest-rate environment has a key benefit: you can get stuck into paying off your principal quickly as the interest doesn't accrue as fast. As a frugalista, I love a bargain, and paying off a mortgage at bargain prices is a good deal to me.

I suggest that whenever interest rates go down, you continue making repayments at the same level as previously. In fact, it's a good idea to repay your mortgage at a rate a few percentage points higher than your actual rate so that if there are interest rate hikes, you'll be prepared with a buffer.

Summary

- Compound interest is mathematical magic. Once you understand how it works, it will rock your world.
- A dollar is worth more than a dollar if you use it to pay back debt (or invest it). That dollar is gone if you spend it, and it could even cost you more if you're using credit.
- The compounding effect means that if you pay only the minimum amount on your credit card, it will take you many years to pay the money back – and you'll pay a lot of interest.
- The same concept works with your mortgage, which is why you will save on interest and own your home sooner if you pay more.
- You will need to pay $6661 a month to pay off a $600,000 loan at 6 per cent interest in 10 years. That sounds like a lot, but even small amounts paid regularly will have a big impact on your mortgage over time.
- Whether you are in a high- or low-interest-rate environment, paying your mortgage off is a low-risk investment.

Now that you know how compound interest affects you and how you might approach paying your mortgage off in high- and low-interest-rate environments, it's time to get to work. In the next couple of chapters I'm going to look at setting goals and explore the strategies you can use to reach them.

Chapter 4

Goal-setting and mindset strategies to reduce your mortgage

In earlier chapters, we looked at how compound interest works and why paying off your mortgage is a good strategy. I will offer a series of financial hacks to help you pay your mortgage quickly in the next chapter, but first I'm going to lay the foundations for success with some specific mindset strategies and approaches that will help you reach your goal of paying your mortgage off quickly.

Make being mortgage free your priority

The key to smashing your mortgage is one word: priority. If you make paying your mortgage off your priority, you are more likely to achieve your goal. That sounds obvious, but there are many other things that can keep you from making your mortgage your priority. For instance, some new home owners also want to get married, go on holidays, renovate their home and socialise with their friends. Then there are all the consumer temptations to deal with every day, from coffees and bagels to clothing and tech toys.

We've discussed why paying your mortgage off quickly is the best financial strategy, but it's easy to succumb to doubt – particularly when other people share their blingy investment successes, from crypto to forex trading – and begin to feel that your strategy is old-school or conservative. However, in my experience there is nothing like the power of a clear goal to drive investment success. So, set your financial goal and then work to follow it (more on that in just a moment). Once you've achieved your goal and have the stability of home ownership behind you, you'll be better placed to experiment with other investment strategies.

How does making your mortgage a priority look in practice? In 2016, I was close to being mortgage free on my house, the former family home, and was super focused on achieving my goal of paying off my home loan within the year (which I did). I remember talking to a similarly frugal friend about how I was prioritising reaching my goal over making everyday purchases.

'Recently, I was at ALDI and saw a lovely doona set,' I told her. 'I picked it up, looked at it and imagined it on my bed. Then I looked at the price. $60! I decided that paying off my mortgage was more important, so I put it back. Then I went and transferred $60 onto my mortgage.'

My friend was amazed.

'I would have just bought the doona,' she said.

Setting myself the goal of paying my mortgage off within the year, and then making that goal a priority over purchasing things I didn't really need (such as flash doonas, chai lattes and so on), was an incredibly effective strategy for catching money leaks and eliminating distraction. Could you do the same?

Chunk it down

Neil and I usually sit down together in January and work out our financial goals for the year ahead. This year is a bit unusual as we are facing a lot of change: Neil's about to retire, and I've just gone back to full-time work in the public service. That's just it: things change. It's easy to lose your way when life changes, so chunking down a big goal, like paying off your mortgage, into smaller progress goals is a powerful way of staying motivated and on track (especially when you're close to reaching your goal). While most people prefer to set goals they know they can easily reach, I believe in setting slightly higher goals that make me work just a little bit harder. This is important to me, as it motivates me to really give it my all.

Setting monthly and yearly mortgage goals is similar, in ways, to the process of writing this book. The book didn't write itself – and nor will your mortgage pay itself! Before I even started writing, I sat down and worked out a chapter plan. I decided not only what I was going to write about but also how many words I would write each week. As is my usual approach, I aimed for more than was strictly necessary to reach my goal on time. With my deadline in mind, I worked backwards on a plan to make it happen. Little by little, big things get done – even if it does feel daunting or even impossible at first. This book is testament to that, as will be your mortgage when you make that final payment.

Try neurolinguistic programming

Having a goal is one thing. Committing to it and making it happen is another. You don't want paying off your mortgage to be another New Year's resolution that doesn't last beyond the first week. One of the keys to achieving goals is keeping them front of mind. When you are focused on something and think about it often, you are more likely to prioritise making it happen. You may find it effective to use neurolinguistic programming (NLP) techniques as a way of amplifying your focus on your goal.

The idea behind using NLP to pay off your mortgage is to use your personal learning preference to motivate you to achieve your goal. Around 70 per cent of people are visual learners, which is why social media apps such as Instagram are so popular. Around 20 per cent are auditory learners, which means that sound is most important to them. Auditory people often love listening to music and podcasts. The remainder are kinaesthetic learners, meaning they prefer to do and feel things. Are you more visual, auditory or kinaesthetic?

If you prefer a visual learning style, you could use visual stimuli to help you focus on your goal. For example, you could make a vision board featuring a picture of a house and the words 'mortgage free'. You could print out graphs and stick them next to your desk at work or on your fridge. Or you could create a graphic about your mortgage goal using Canva and make it your computer or phone background. The key is making sure you *see* and *notice* your goal regularly. When you see it, take a moment to visualise yourself achieving your goal. The more often you do this, the more you will stay focused and on track.

If you prefer an auditory approach, you might achieve better results by reciting your goals aloud. In *Think and Grow Rich*, Napoleon Hill recommends people read their goals aloud every night before they go to sleep. As they read, they can think deeply about their goal and visualise it happening. In this context, saying something like 'I will own my home outright by Christmas 2030' each night could help you focus and motivate you towards reaching your goal.

Kinaesthetic learners, in contrast, need to feel connected to their goals. I'm a kinaesthetic learner, and I know how important it is to feel your goal. If this is you too, you can try using a combination of the strategies I suggested for visual and auditory learners, but I would encourage you also to do things that replicate the feeling of accomplishing your goal. For instance, you may wish to draw up a mock bank statement and rip it up, imaging as you do that it's your mortgage. You could also walk into the office of your lender (or call them) to ask about the process of discharging your mortgage. Alternatively, you could start planning an amazing mortgage-free party by writing down ideas and people to invite.

Hit your mortgage hard – and early

The more extra payments you can make against your mortgage, especially early on, the better your financial position will be. As I discussed in chapters 2 and 3, the quicker you can reduce your total loan, the better you can minimise the compounding effect. You probably won't see the benefits of this for some time, and it may even feel like you aren't making a dent, but what you do early on has a huge impact over the life of your loan.

Additionally, if you put extra money into your mortgage early you will also build up an emergency fund. Taking on the responsibility of a mortgage is a large commitment. If something unexpected happens – say, a pandemic, a redundancy or an accident that leaves you unable to work for a few months – you will have a buffer to cover you. Don't think it won't happen to you; it could, and it's important to hope for the best but plan for the worst.

Catch the windfalls

Have you ever had an unexpected windfall? Maybe you won the Melbourne Cup sweep, received an inheritance or even got a Medicare refund. Or perhaps you received a better-than-expected tax refund or bonus at work. Whatever the source, make sure your windfall goes straight to the mortgage. It can be tempting to view this unexpected income as a sign to go out and enjoy your life. Yes, it is important to enjoy your life, but if you didn't miss the windfall before it suddenly appeared, you won't miss it if you put it straight on your mortgage. You will be able to plan for an amazing celebration once that mortgage is paid.

Live on one wage

If you're in a relationship, consider working together to pay your mortgage. Living on one wage and saving and investing the second wage is a great way to turbo-charge your finances. It's an especially good strategy if you're planning to start a family, as it prepares you for what life might be like if one partner plans to take time off work for a while or become a stay-at-home parent. This strategy requires a high degree of trust, especially if the home was purchased by one member of the partnership prior to you coming together. You're going to need to have some honest money conversations – and it's probably best to have them early.

I married Neil in 2018. It was second time lucky for both of us. Prior to getting married we discussed whether to enter into a binding financial agreement, also known as a pre-nup, but decided against it. Instead, we took the risk of combining our finances. I purchased my apartment six months prior to meeting Neil and had a small mortgage. He moved in, and we decided it made more sense to focus on paying off my mortgage than for him to pay rent. I say 'my' because the unit was, and is, in my name. In the leadup to this decision, we tracked our spending as a couple using the Splitwise app (there are several out there now, such as Settle Up). This helped to instil trust in each other and confirmed that we had similar money values in addition to our similar incomes. On balance – and having done the sums to ensure that one salary would cover our combined living expenses – we felt that living on one income and investing the other made sense. It certainly enabled us to pay off the mortgage faster than I could have with my income alone. It effectively gave us double the financial power.

Look beyond your local and avoid the loyalty tax

I'm always shocked when I hear that people have settled on a home loan just because it was offered by the bank at their local shopping centre. Having your bank near where you live is not the convenience you might expect. Typically, the only reason you should need to contact your bank is to request a rate review (more on that in the next chapter), and even then you probably still won't visit the branch in person, because most rate review requests are handled by specialist divisions that you can only contact by phone or email. If you're paying your mortgage when it's due, even making additional repayments, you'll likely never speak to anyone at your bank. If you're experiencing financial hardship, that's a whole other issue. I talk about this in chapter 16.

People are brand loyal. Once we choose a brand we like, we tend to stick with it – especially when it's a bank. But, just because you like a certain bank, it doesn't mean it likes you. Maybe you get exceptional customer service and have your own private banker but, in most cases, banks don't know you. You're just a number. Despite this, the big banks earn around $4.5 billion each year from customer loyalty, unearned though it may be. This is known as 'the loyalty tax'. To attract new customers, banks need to spend money on marketing and other costs, and offer attractive 'front book' loans. They often do this by charging existing 'back book' customers more. On average, new customers obtain mortgage rates that are 86 basis points lower than existing customers. According to one report, assuming a $500,000 loan, an existing loyal customer would pay on average $70,000 more over the life of their loan – assuming they don't get a rate review (more on that in the next chapter).

Summary

- If you make paying off your mortgage your priority, you are less likely to get distracted by other destinations for your money – be that 'sure thing' investments, impulse purchases or money leaks.

- Looking at the entire amount you have to repay can be daunting. Break it down into smaller chunks by setting goals to work towards.

- Are you a visual, auditory or kinaesthetic learner? Try using neurolinguistic programming techniques to focus and motivate you towards your goal.

- Put any financial windfalls straight onto your mortgage.

- If you are in a relationship characterised by deep trust – and you can afford it – consider living on one wage and using the other to pay off your mortgage.

- Don't automatically go with your local bank. Instead, shop around to find the best deal on your mortgage.

Armed with these goal-setting and mindset strategies, it's time to take action. The next chapter offers helpful hints for getting the best possible deal on your mortgage and sets you up with financial hacks that will make a real difference to your bottom line.

Chapter 5

Finance hacks for repaying your mortgage fast

Paying your mortgage off ahead of the typical 30 years offered by lenders takes commitment and focus. Before I take you through some extra ways of saving money to use on paying your mortgage – beyond living off baked beans – here are some finance hacks that, paired with the mindset strategies of chapter 4, will set you up to achieve your home-ownership goals.

Get the best deal

The basic premise for success is that the smaller the debt, the lower the interest rate and the shorter the term, the sooner you will pay off your loan. I've already mentioned a few strategies that will help you achieve those key goals, but it all begins with ensuring you have the best deal on your mortgage. Let's talk about that.

Negotiate a lower interest rate

When was the last time you rang your lender and asked for a better deal? Wait, you can do that? Yes, you most certainly can! I did recently and immediately got 80 basis points (0.8 per cent) off the variable rate.

I'm one of the 800,000 people who fixed their mortgage when rates were low in 2021 and 2022 (more about fixing – or not fixing – your rate later in this chapter), at least on my investment properties. So, when those loans reverted to the standard variable rate (SVR), I researched the rates offered at other institutions. Armed with that information, I then rang my non-bank lender. The person I spoke with was super helpful. It wasn't stressful, and it wasn't difficult. I had four loans with them, and they wanted to retain my business, so they offered me a better deal.

This is a common experience. According to Lendi chief executive David Hyman, most banks will give customers a better deal when they ring. As he said in an interview with *The Australian Financial Review*, 'Banks are eyes wide open to the challenge; those that call will get the best outcomes, and those that don't will get the SVR and the loyalty tax will still exist … It makes sense to shop around.'

Consider switching lenders

If your lender isn't providing you with a competitive interest rate and isn't willing to budge, you have the option to switch lenders. At the time of writing, lenders are offering competitive rates – they're hungry for your business.

According to the ABS, new loan commitments for housing fell by 5.3 per cent in January 2023. At the same time, business construction loans fell by 2.5 per cent. Also, the value of new borrower-accepted loan commitments fell by 35 per cent for owner occupiers, with investor loans falling by 34.8 per cent. This is a huge drop from just months before when the property boom was reaching its peak. In such an environment, illustrated in figure 4, mortgage lenders fall over themselves to attract new business. Several lenders even offered new customers cash payments of $3000 to switch their loans over to them.

Figure 4: Lending indicators – new loan commitments, total housing in Australia

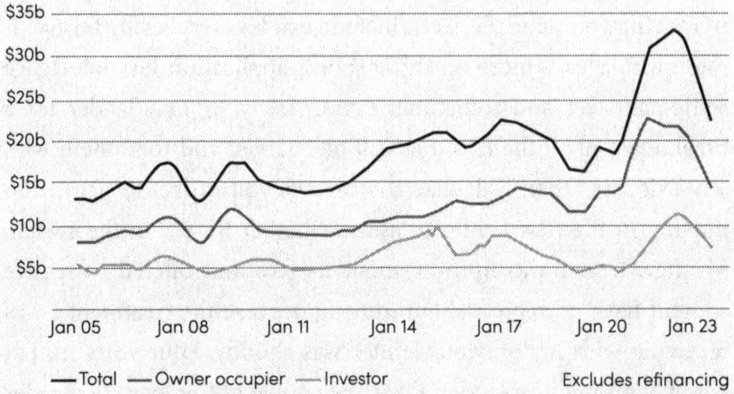

(SOURCE: ABS)

It's easy to compare lenders. You can ask a mortgage broker for assistance or use one of the many online finance comparison sites, such as Canstar, InfoChoice, Finder, Compare the Market and RateCity. Note that many of these sites do not compare all brands – this is because, as they are not government sites, they may make money through advertising and commissions. You can also ask money-savvy friends who they use and if they are happy with their provider. They might surprise you with a refer-a-friend deal.

Be aware, too, that there are often unforeseen costs in switching. I switched lenders a few years ago after discovering a large, hidden annual fee. I tried several times to talk to my lender, but the representative either didn't turn up at the appointed time, turned up late or 'mansplained' to me. So, I switched. However, I discovered that moving was much more difficult and expensive than I had foreseen. It ended up costing me thousands of dollars in unexpected exit fees, settlement fees and other charges across several loans – something I was interviewed about in *The Australian Financial Review* – not to mention the hours and hours spent filling out forms and providing corroborating details and identification.

Before you switch, make sure you calculate all the fees involved in moving your loan. Fees can include exit fees (especially for fixed-rate mortgages – more on those soon), application fees, mortgage settlement fees and sometimes taxes. Ask your new lender for a breakdown of all the fees that will be charged and total them with any exit fees. Then, calculate the savings you expect to gain from moving to the new lender to assess whether it's worth the switch. My new lender was upfront about its fees and offered to reduce some. I have no regrets about moving because the treatment I was receiving with my previous lender was shoddy. Four years in, I'm happy with my new lender. Over the course of the loan, I consider the benefits of switching will far outweigh the costs.

Though it can be hard to work out when rates are changing, you must do the maths to determine how much better off you will be if you switch lenders. Cheap lenders may tempt you with low interest rates to begin with, but they can then become uncompetitive over time and more expensive in the long run. My advice is to instead choose a lender with a good track record of favourable rates, and then let the miracle of compound interest will work in your favour.

If you do decide to move, when your lender receives your discharge authority form a member of their sales team will usually contact you to offer a better deal. It's your choice whether to stay with a lender who didn't value you until you were nearly out the door or to go with a new lender.

Optimise your credit score

Whether you're negotiating with your current lender or thinking about switching, one of the best ways to get an optimal interest rate is to be someone a lender wants. When you apply for a job, you ensure your CV and LinkedIn profile look good. You might even try to get extra experience or training to help you take the next step in your career. Similarly, you also need to spend time making sure you look mortgage-worthy.

The best deals are available to borrowers with good credit ratings. Look at it from a lender's perspective. They want to know that you can pay your mortgage off. So, their ideal candidate is someone with a stable, permanent job, a history of paying back debt commitments and a good savings history – and before they approve a loan, they will run a credit check on the applicant.

Want to know what your credit score is? You can run one online. I used the tool on the Canstar website to run a check on myself. As you might expect from the author of this book, my score was 'Excellent' at 1004 points (figure 5) – two points higher than my husband!

Figure 5: My credit score

The good news is, wherever you are on the scale, you can improve your score. Four key factors contribute to your credit rating:

1. existing home loans and home loan applications
2. employment and residential stability

3. rare or infrequent loan applications
4. strong credit history.

Let's start with existing home loans and applications. If you already have a home loan and are paying it off regularly, it helps your credit score. I know that sounds odd – needing to have a mortgage to get a good credit rating to get a mortgage – but if there is no data on which to assess you, it is hard to give you a reliable score. In practice, this may mean that you get a mortgage at an ordinary rate, and then have to negotiate a better deal after demonstrating your ability pay it.

Second on the list is stable employment and residence. A solid, permanent job and residence in the same place for many years are considered positives. This is because a lender doesn't want to lend to someone whose financial situation is always changing or who looks like they could be running away from debt. If you have your own business, change jobs or move around a lot (due to a defence career, for example), it may be hard to do well in this criterion, but it's not the end of the world. You may just need to focus on the other three factors to bring your score up.

Now let's return to loan applications and credit. As I've noted, having a mortgage (or a credit card) can support a higher credit score because it shows you can manage debt responsibly. On the other hand, constantly transferring credit cards to new deals or being knocked back for loans are red flags. There are three things to keep in mind here if you want to improve your credit score:

1. Don't fill out multiple mortgage forms. It can look like you are shopping around after being knocked back even if it isn't the case. It's fine to discuss your options with multiple lenders, but don't go the whole way with them. If you have a broker, they will work to identify the best lender so you don't have to worry as much about the risk to your credit rating.

2. Watch your credit card limits – they matter more than how much you owe on your credit card. When my friend Dan went for a loan, his credit card with a $5000 limit reduced his borrowing capacity by $40,000. This is because lenders assessed it on the worst-case scenario of that credit card being maxed out and interest compounding.

3. For those who have graduated from university or another tertiary institution, a HECS-HELP loan could also adversely affect your borrowing capacity. This is because lenders will look at your debt liabilities to assess how much they can give you based on your perceived ability to service a loan. If you have a large HECS-HELP debt, it could make it harder for you to service a loan.

Finally, it's a good idea to do everything you can to maintain a strong credit history. One of the best ways you can do this is to pay your bills on time. Even better, pay them early. Whenever I receive my credit card statement, I immediately schedule a payment online for a few days before it's due. Then I pay the amount in full. I automate other bills whenever possible. I also have a folder where I put copies of all paper bills. Each month has a plastic sleeve where I put the bills, with a bill summary that includes the amount, payee and due date on the front.

Paying your bills on time might seem like a little thing. However, your integrity will be rewarded with an excellent credit score and, therefore, the ability to negotiate the best possible deal on your mortgage.

Figure out whether fixing is right for you

One of the most significant decisions you will need to make as a home owner is whether to fix the interest rate on your mortgage.

Are you the sort of person who hates numbers and turns the TV off when the finance report comes on? Do you ever stop to listen to what the Reserve Bank says about interest rates? Do you even know when the Reserve Bank will be meeting? Or do you switch off? Once you are a home owner with a mortgage, if you do nothing else, make sure you stay informed about the general state of the domestic and international economy and how that might affect interest rates.

Having a fixed interest rate on your loan means that the rate at which interest is charged remains the same for a certain period of time, usually from one to five years. That means that whether the variable interest rate at your lender goes up or down, you will still be charged the same rate of interest on that loan.

As was the case for around 800,000 other Australian households in 2021, I fixed the interest rates on my mortgages when they were at record lows. At the time, people were talking about how interest rates might even go to zero, so fixing was considered a bit of a risk. As it happened, interest rates went up, but they could have gone down.

When interest rates were falling, people with fixed rates found themselves paying tens of thousands more in interest than if they had stayed with a variable rate. You might wonder why they didn't cut their losses and get out of that deal. Unfortunately, it's not that simple. Fixed rates are just that – fixed. There are usually penalties, known as 'break fees', for ending a fixed-rate loan early. When I refinanced three of my investment properties and put them on a fixed rate, the terms of the contract allowed me to pay no more than $10,000 extra per year per loan. If I chose to sell one of those properties while under that fixed loan contract, I would have had to pay break fees.

Splitting your loan is one way to ensure a degree of certainty while also retaining the flexibility to make additional repayments and take advantage of possible falling interest rates. Splitting your loan means fixing a portion of it and leaving the rest at a variable rate. This allows you to plough through and repay the variable part while having the security of knowing that interest rates won't soar to alarmingly high levels.

Decisions to fix often come from a place of fear. What if rates get so high that you can't afford to pay them? What if you can't pay? I can't say we will never again experience 17.5 per cent interest rates as we did in 1990, but I do want to suggest that fear-based decisions are rarely the best. If you follow the tips that I offer in this book and you make additional repayments, you are less likely to lose your home if interest rates go up. Additionally, if you are struggling, I have some ideas for you to consider in part II.

My approach is to always go for the lower rate. Always. I don't know what will happen in the future, so if something is a good deal now, I'll take it, thank you very much. As my strategy is to pay off loans quickly, especially if that loan is for my home, I usually prefer a standard variable rate as there are no limitations on making additional repayments. That said, if there was a special deal on fixed rates that suited me – as there was in 2021 when I refinanced the investment properties I mentioned earlier – I'd take it in a flash and park any additional money in other investments until needed.

Pay fortnightly

One of the easiest ways to get ahead on your mortgage is to pay fortnightly. Yes, fortnightly. Finance writer Noel Whittaker popularised this strategy with his book *Making Money Made Simple*.

As I detailed in chapters 2 and 3, the monthly repayment on a $600,000 loan at 6 per cent per annum over a 30-year term is $3597. However, if you pay half of that ($1798.50) each fortnight, your loan will be paid off in 24 years and seven months – over five years ahead of schedule. Plus, you'll save $148,342 in interest.

How does it work? Though there are 12 months in a year, there are 26 fortnights. So, if you pay half the monthly repayments fortnightly, you'll end up making an additional month's worth of mortgage payments a year, and that adds up over the life of your loan. You're likely to quickly get into the habit of paying fortnightly and adjust your spending accordingly. You may not even notice you're paying a bit more each year – especially if you get paid fortnightly – and, as you'll remember from chapter 3, paying faster and more frequently also helps to reduce interest charges.

Note that while some lenders now offer fortnightly payments, their calculations don't lead to additional repayments. This is because, rather than dividing the monthly amount by two, they take the annual fee and divide it by 26. Counter this by doing your own maths and setting your own fortnightly mortgage payments.

Use an offset account

When you apply for your home loan, you'll probably hear about whizz-bang features such as offset accounts. Offset accounts are like bank accounts, except they're attached to your mortgage. The general premise is that instead of earning interest on your savings – and paying tax on it – you get a reduction on the interest charges on your mortgage.

For instance, say that you have $20,000 sitting in your offset account rather than in a savings account. That $20,000 is equivalent to 6 per cent tax free (assuming you're reducing your $600,000 mortgage by $20,000 at 6 per cent). Depending on your savings account, you might otherwise earn 4 per cent interest (in many cases less). You would also pay tax on that interest as it is an investment. Lenders offering offset accounts like to spruik their benefits.

For instance, according to Orange Finance, $20,000 sitting in a $500,000 loan account would save you two years off the life of the loan and over $62,000 in interest.

Using an offset account is convenient because, although it's much like a standard bank account, moving money to and from your mortgage is easier, meaning it's also simpler to make additional repayments. If you plan to use an offset account, you may wish to close other savings accounts and instead use your offset for your day-to-day banking. The idea is that ensuring your pay or other income goes into this account allows you to maximise interest savings.

Though I've used an offset account before, I don't anymore. I prefer to keep my accounts separate, and mortgages with offset accounts are often (though not always) more expensive. Instead, my approach is now to get a low-interest-rate mortgage with zero fees. So long as it meets those criteria and has an easy-to-use redraw facility, I don't care if my mortgage has all the bells and whistles.

Consider living on a credit card

Credit cards are evil and wrong. Right? Recently, I was watching the 2009 film *Confessions of a Shopaholic*. Rebecca Bloomwood, played by Australian actress Isla Fisher, was addicted to buying designer clothing and in serious financial distress. She had frozen her credit card in a large block of ice as part of her commitment to getting out of debt, but when she heard about a designer sale, she hacked at the block of ice until she could free the credit card and go shopping.

If you can relate to that experience, then using your credit card as part of your strategy to pay your mortgage off early is not likely to be a good idea for you. If, however, you regularly exercise fiscal restraint, this can work a treat. It's what we do, and it has helped us afford some awesome international travel (more on that in chapter 15).

This is how it works:

1. Apply for a credit card with a low annual fee and a good rewards program. Don't worry about a low interest rate (the idea is to pay it off in full at the end of each month), but do make sure it offers a good interest-free period, ideally 55 days.
2. Choose a mortgage with a fee-free, easy-to-use redraw facility (or offset account).
3. Deposit your pay straight into your mortgage account. You will use this like a bank account – sort of.
4. Use your credit card for everyday expenses such as groceries, dining out and paying bills where possible and practical. Make sure you take notice of any fees you might incur for using your card; sometimes it isn't worth the interest savings if you're paying hefty bank merchant fees.
5. Pay your credit card in full every month. As soon as you get your credit card statement, schedule to pay it in full using your redraw facility.

This system hinges on using your credit card's interest-free period to your advantage, allowing you to slightly reduce the interest paid on your mortgage because you're leaving more cash in your account. As a bonus, depending on the card you select, you can also receive rewards points on credit card purchases, which you can use for fun things such as travel and gifts.

One disadvantage of this approach is that it can be difficult to see the true value of your mortgage. As you are often withdrawing from your account, your true mortgage balance is less clear, and it can be less motivating than if you instead have a separate mortgage account that you can see decrease consistently.

It's important to note that this strategy will only work if you manage your credit card well. You will probably need to set a budget and monitor it carefully. Before adopting this approach, I suggest trying other methods of paying your mortgage. If you do give it a go, monitor your success, and check in at 3, 6 and 12 months to see if it's still a good strategy for you. If your credit card is getting out of hand, you can always freeze it in a block of ice.

Summary

- Contact your lender and request a rate review. They are unlikely to shame you or treat you like Oliver Twist for daring to ask.

- If your lender doesn't offer you a sufficiently large discount, or doesn't treat you well when you ask, it's time to think about switching. Note that switching will involve costs, and you will also have to spend time filling out forms. However, it can be worth it if you are able to lock in a good deal.

- Explore ways of improving your credit rating. A good rating will help you get a better deal on your mortgage.

- Divide your monthly payment by two and pay that amount each fortnight. This trick alone will help you achieve home ownership years sooner – and save you paying interest.

- Consider whether to fix your mortgage rate or negotiate a split loan with your lender. Note that there may be break costs if you sell your home or refinance before the term ends, as well as limits on how much you can repay within the period.

- Look into living on your credit card. This means depositing all of your pay into your mortgage account, using your credit card for living expenses whenever practical and then paying it in full before the end of the interest-free period using your mortgage's redraw facility.

In the first five chapters I have taken you through the benefits of being mortgage free and set out mindset and financial strategies that will get you there. Now it's time to help you find more money for your mortgage so you can reach your home-ownership goals. You might even surprise yourself with how much you're able to save.

PART II

MORE MONEY FOR THE MORTGAGE

Chapter 6

Insurance audit

When focusing on paying off your mortgage, it can be easy to get stuck on the money you can save in the short term. However, life is uncertain, and there are risks that could not just derail your mortgage-free dreams but also cause you serious financial harm. I'm not a licensed financial planner and I can't give you financial advice, but I suggest that you do obtain financial advice from a financial planner, especially in terms of potential risks to you and your loved ones, to ensure that you covered for the unexpected.

In this chapter, I will cover some different kinds of insurance that you may need to consider as part of your overarching financial plan. Remember, it's important to do your research and ensure you make the right choice for your specific needs and circumstances. Finance publications can be good places to start, and some give out awards for high-quality products in the finance space, including for insurance. For instance, *Money* has an annual 'Best of the Best' edition. While things change, the products featured have generally undergone a high degree of scrutiny, making these lists good places to start when comparing products.

Health insurance

Do you have health insurance? Do you need it? These are very important questions. Private health insurance is expensive – I pay more on health insurance than I do to insure my properties – and if you think it has been getting more expensive, you'd be right. On average, premiums have increased by more than 50 per cent in a decade, and in 2023 the average increase was 2.9 per cent.

There have been times when my family and I have had urgent, lifesaving treatment without needing private health insurance. I had urgent surgery for a ruptured appendix when I was a teenager. My eldest son was born two months premature, was not expected to live and had to be in the neonatal intensive care unit for weeks. My husband received urgent care after having a massive heart attack. These interventions were all covered by our public health system. So, why do we still have private health insurance? Well, back in 2007 I needed urgent neurosurgery a week before Christmas. My preferred neurosurgeon only worked through the private system. That's just it: if you have private health insurance, you can have more choice in your treatment.

There are a lot of things that aren't optimal with Australia's health system, and that includes the cost of private health insurance. For home owners wanting to pay down their mortgage, whether to take out or continue with private health insurance is a big decision. Before you make that choice, there are a few things to consider.

If you are over 30 years of age, private health insurance may become more expensive due to lifetime health cover (LHC) loading. This government policy means that you pay an additional 2 per cent premium (up to 70 per cent) for every year you haven't held hospital cover from the year you turn 31. The good news is that the LHC is removed after you've held hospital cover for 10 continuous years. The bad news is that you can't just stop and start insurance – you may become liable to pay the LHC loading again if you take out another private patient hospital cover later.

If you are earning a good income you may also have to pay the Medicare levy surcharge, in addition to the normal Medicare levy, if you don't have private hospital insurance. There are several tiers of payment for singles and families depending on their income and dependents, but to illustrate, a single person who earned $140,001 or more in the 2022–23 income year would have paid an additional levy of up to 1.5 per cent if they didn't have private health insurance for that period. Accordingly, many people opt for a simple hospital cover (not extras) as this can be a similar price as, and sometimes cheaper than, paying the levy surcharge at their income level. If you decide to not take out hospital cover, think carefully about ambulance cover (if available), as in many states and territories calling an ambulance is more expensive than you might think. In the ACT it costs $1032 (+$14 per kilometre over the border) if you're not insured, but ambulance call-outs are included in most private hospital insurance covers. You never want to have to hesitate about calling an ambulance due to the cost.

If you do have or take out private health insurance, it's important to regularly check you're getting a good deal. According to Choice, you could save up to $935 a year by switching policies. There are several commercial comparison sites you can use, but I like privatehealth.gov.au, which is government supported. Some schemes are not open to the public (for example, Defence Health, Reserve Bank Health Society and Teachers Health), but you might be surprised by what you are eligible to join. If you do switch funds, you won't need to re-serve waiting periods you have qualified for, but it's important to compare levels of cover to make sure you have what you need. Remember, the important date for switching is 1 April, as that's when premiums generally go up each year. Sometimes, if premiums are going up steeply, it might be worth paying the premium in full for the next year in advance of 1 April so that you can pay it at a lower rate. However, you'll need to compare this to the cost saving you would make if you used that money to pay down your mortgage more quickly.

Another option is setting up your own health scheme. This means putting aside the money you would have spent on private health insurance and instead investing it yourself (including making additional repayments on your mortgage). The advantage of this approach is having control over your own money, but the disadvantage is that your own funds might not be enough if you need expensive medical treatment, and you may not be able to access your preferred provider when you need to. You may also have to pay the Medicare levy surcharge, and LHC loading would also still apply.

Potential savings – ditching your insurance:

Per year (minus Medicare levy surcharge)	$1920
Time saved on your mortgage	3 years and 2 months
Interest saved on your mortgage	$88,270

Potential savings – switching to a cheaper fund or policy:

Per year	$935
Time saved on your mortgage	1 year and 8 months
Interest saved on your mortgage	$46,390

Life insurance and income protection insurance

Think you'll always be able to work in a stable full-time job and you'll always be able to pay your mortgage? Your health might have other ideas. A few days before Christmas in 2017, Neil had a heart attack. Six months, four stents and some complications later, he started rehab. In his rehab class was another heart attack patient who had been in intensive care at the same time. He was alive, but the family finances were foundering as he was too unwell to go back to work. Don't let this happen to you. You never know what is going to happen, and you need to protect yourself and your family.

I am considering life insurance and income protection insurance together in this chapter, but it's important to note that they are not the same. In fact, there are several different types of insurance that can provide cover for you and your family in the case of death or injury, and this is something to consider when talking to a financial planner.

Simply put, life insurance relates to what others get when you die or you're diagnosed as terminally ill. You need to be clear about your beneficiaries and ensure you are adequately covered so that your family is provided for if something happens to you. Sadly, things do happen – and it's often unexpected. It's especially important to consider life insurance if you have vulnerable dependants, such as young children or a spouse who might struggle to support the family without you. Income protection insurance, on the other hand, covers you if something unexpected happens and you can't work. For instance, if you are involved in an accident or experience illness and are unable to go back to work, income protection insurance ensures you still have some money coming in.

Before you consider purchasing a commercial insurance product, first see what your superannuation offers. Though the focus tends to be on performance, superannuation funds also generally offer life, total and permanent disability, and income protection insurance for members. Sometimes that insurance is very generous – and sometimes less so. It's useful to know what you already have before you go out and buy a whole new policy. You can also consider topping it up through your superannuation, but do be aware that this could result in less money going to work in building up your super balance. It's also important to note that superannuation funds cancel insurance on inactive accounts after 16 months to prevent inactive accounts being charged fees for services they don't need (for example, when someone has multiple accounts they haven't combined). If you take time out from the workforce, such as for caring responsibilities or mid-career study, it's important to understand that insurance on your superannuation may be paused.

Beware, too, of signing up to schemes you see spruiked on daytime television or in magazines. If an insurance provider needs to spend big on emotive ad campaigns, it's best to proceed with caution. Always read the product disclosure statement and contract to understand what you're getting into, and carefully compare products before you sign. (Moneysmart has a good tool for this.)

Also, consider whether you need life or income protection insurance at all. *But Serina, didn't you just spend a whole lot of time talking about the risks of not having insurance?* Yes, but everyone's situation is different. For instance, Neil's heart attack did not set him back financially. He had spent nearly 30 years in the public service and had over two years of sick leave entitlements, which allowed him to take several months off and gradually return to work. Had he been unable to return to work, he could have accessed his superannuation scheme's disability provisions. If we consider his specific situation, Neil does not currently need any additional insurance. In contrast, if a tradesperson working as a contractor, with a stay-at-home partner and young kids, were injured – or worse – on the job, it would be financially devasting for their family. This is why it's important to get advice about how best to protect your family's interests.

The cost of your cover will depend on how large a benefit you're insured for and how difficult it is to claim due to how disability is defined. If you need to save on premiums, for example, it might be worth having a smaller benefit with higher-quality definitions rather than having more cover that is harder to claim. Also, you don't always need to insure to be in the same position that you would have been in if you didn't fall ill. You might, for example, insure the income you need for the essentials in your budget but leave out the income you need for the luxuries. Once you've made any changes to your finances, it can pay to go back and revisit any decisions you made about how much cover you need.

Home and contents insurance

The rising cost of living is a challenge. Who could have foreseen a global pandemic, fires and floods causing the incredible supply chain issues and price hikes of recent years? It can be tempting to forgo things like insurance when times are tight, but if you don't have home and contents insurance, you are exposed.

The city where I live was covered in a thick haze of smoke for months during the summer bushfires of 2019–20. My home experienced little fire damage, but others nearby weren't so lucky. Overnight, their homes, their businesses and their possessions went up in smoke. Many of these people had moved into smaller towns for affordability reasons and couldn't afford insurance. In addition to the trauma of losing their homes and surviving a fire, they had to grapple with financial hardship to rebuild and restart. Meanwhile, due to their level of cover, others have been able to build back even better than before. Could you afford to rebuild if something like that happened to you?

While politicians argue about whether climate change is real, insurance companies have been increasing premiums in response to frequent and extreme weather events. Choice calculates that the average quotes for combined home and contents insurance premiums in Australia rose by over 72 per cent in the five years from April 2017 to April 2022, an average increase of $1147 per annum. In Western Australia, premiums rose by 101 per cent. People living in high-risk areas are paying more and more for their home and contents insurance; they may not even be able to find an insurance company willing to ensure them at all. According to the Insurance Council of Australia, around 23 per cent of Australians don't have building or contents insurance. This means that around 1.8 million residential households are not protected in the event of property damage. Being without insurance or having to pay expensive premiums is putting many vulnerable people in even more vulnerable positions. If you are looking to purchase a property, make sure to find out if the property is insurable before you purchase it. You don't want to find out after your purchase that you cannot insure what may be your biggest asset due to bushfire or flood zoning.

The risks of going without home and contents insurance are too great to warrant cancelling it to save a few dollars. However, with premiums going up, you need to be savvy to get a good deal. Here are some of my top tips.

Use an insurance broker

Insurance brokers aren't just for businesses. You can save money using them, too, particularly if there are multiple insurance products involved – and chances are you'll need more than one insurance product. For example, Neil and I have landlord insurance, contents insurance for our home, car insurance, insurance for Neil's midlife-crisis motorcycle, insurance for his caravan and professional indemnity insurance for my business. We were amazed when we first started using a broker that the quote for caravan insurance was several hundred dollars cheaper than what we could find online. Furthermore, when we've needed to make claims our broker has been helpful in directing us through the process.

Ask your insurance company for a better deal

Insurance companies typically offer more attractive rates to new customers than to existing customers. They will put up your insurance premium when you renew, then offer a cheaper premium to new customers. If you aren't using a broker, make sure to ring your insurance company before paying to ask it's the best they can do. Do a bit of sleuthing on your product before you pay, too. An easy way to do this is by performing an internet search as if you are a new customer, perhaps even using a different name and address, and the incognito mode on your browser. If you can get a better deal as a new customer, make sure to let your insurer know.

Shop around

It's easier than ever to compare different insurance products' value for money. Financial comparison sites such as Canstar, Finder and Compare the Market allow you to compare products, and Choice has a home and contents insurance comparison tool as well as some useful guides for getting the best deal. Use these tools for background research, but ensure you make your own inquiries and read the fine print.

Make your home secure

Having good security features in your property, such as security screens and alarm systems, can result in a decrease in premiums. Making these upgrades can save you in the long run; even simple window locks can save you money.

Insure for the right amount

It's important to insure your home and contents for the right amount. In a property market that can rise – and fall – rapidly, this can be harder than you might realise. If you over-insure your property, you'll pay unnecessarily high premiums. As insurance companies don't like properties to be over-insured because of the risk of fraudulent claims, you are more likely to be underinsured; according to the Australian Securities and Investments Commission, up to 80 per cent of home owners are. This means that around 80 per cent of home owners will not have sufficient insurance to rebuild or repair damage. It's important to monitor the cost of housing in your area and have a good idea of the general cost of rebuilding. A broker can also provide advice based on similar property types.

Increase your excess

When you make a claim, you will generally have to pay an amount in excess. This means that if something happens (for example, your home is broken into), you will have to pay an amount out of pocket before you can claim money back. You can usually pay less in premiums if you undertake to pay more out of pocket if you make a claim.

Car insurance

If you drive a car, you need insurance. Even if you don't drive regularly or think you don't need it, in Australia it's a legal requirement to have compulsory third party (CTP) insurance when you register your vehicle. Comprehensive car insurance, however, is optional, and not everyone has it. If you can afford it, it is important as it will cover your car even if you are at fault.

Last year, our car was badly damaged after Neil hit a kangaroo when was driving home late from a Rural Fire Service brigade committee meeting. The car needed extensive work, but thankfully, other than the excess, it was all covered by our comprehensive car insurance policy.

Many of the tips I shared for reducing the cost of home and contents insurance also apply to car insurance. For instance, you can use a broker to get a deal on comprehensive car insurance. You can also call your insurer, shop around and consider increasing your excess. However, with car insurance, there are a few additional things you can do to reduce your premiums.

Drive carefully

Most insurers will offer a no-claim discount or safe driver bonus to people who rarely make claims. This means that if you never get into accidents, make claims or get tickets for traffic infringements, you are likely to pay a lower premium. It mightn't seem sexy to drive within the speed limit, but being a careful driver is good for your finances – and it might even save your life. While you can't help the stupidity of others on the road, you can learn to anticipate the unexpected by taking a defensive driving course.

Consider who's insured to drive your car

Insurers tend to charge men aged 25 and younger higher premiums. This is because, statistically, younger people – and young men in particular – are riskier drivers and are more likely to be involved in serious crashes than older people. If you have more than one driver on your policy, it's worth being aware of the age and gender factor.

Choose a vehicle that is cheap to insure

You can save on insurance by purchasing a vehicle that your mates might think is uncool. Vehicles that insurers consider to be safe (in other words, not likely to be driven too fast or stolen) are usually cheaper to insure.

My parents drove a Volvo back when it was cool and before the make became the butt of jokes, but cars with good safety features – like many Volvos – have the last laugh when it comes to insurance. Cars with higher safety ratings as determined by the Australasian New Car Assessment Program (ANCAP) usually have lower premiums, so it pays to consider this before buying a vehicle.

Cars with low theft ratings also generally have lower insurance premiums. According to Canstar, in 2022 passenger cars with the lowest risk of theft included Volkswagen Up AA (2012–14), Ford Focus SA (2018+), Toyota Camry GSV70R (2017+), Ford Everest UA (2015+) and Tesla Model S (2014+). Before you make your choice, jump onto the Canstar website to see how the make and model of any car you're interested in stacks up.

Finally, insurance companies tend to charge more to insure the types of cars they think that younger guys are likely to want to drive fast, such as sports cars and sport utes. For example, according to Finder, the average comprehensive insurance policy for Subaru WRX sports car is $148 a month, or $1613 a year (and it would likely cost more if it was driven by a young man in his early 20s). My mother-in-law had a WRX when she was in her 60s (and she was definitely not a fast driver) and even she found the premiums high. Another car that many young men would love to own is a Ford Ranger Raptor 4x4 Ute. According to *Car and Driver*, the average insurance is $110 a month, or $1320 a year, and can go as high as $3210 a year for higher-risk drivers in high-theft areas. Insurance on a Toyota Camry, meanwhile, is less than $1000 a year for most drivers.

DISCLAIMER: Please note that I have not quantified potential savings in the area of insurance cover. How much insurance you take out and what type will depend on your individual circumstances. Saving a dollar in this area of expenditure might not always be the most prudent approach. You should always do your own research and seek your own financial advice.

Summary

- Not only do you need to focus on paying off your mortgage, but you also need to have a risk-mitigation strategy for potential threats. In other words, you need appropriate insurances.

- Private health insurance is becoming increasingly expensive, but it can be useful to ensure you and your family have access to choice of care if you need it – and to avoid the Medicare levy surcharge. If you decide not to take out private health insurance, you may wish to invest in ambulance insurance. (An ambulance ride is free in some states and territories, but it can be expensive in others.)

- Shop around for the best deal, and insure your home for the right amount; you never know when something might happen.

- If you drive a car, you will need car insurance, but a number of things (including your age, your safety record, and the make and model of your car) can influence the cost of your comprehensive car insurance.

Insurance is a good way to protect yourself and your family from the unexpected, but it can be expensive. That's why it's important to make sure all the insurance you hold – including health, life and income protection, home and contents, and car insurance – are appropriate for your specific needs and gives you the best possible value for money. With those bigger-ticket items out of the way, in the next chapter I'm going to help you cut down your weekly food budget without going hungry or resorting to beans on toast.

Chapter 7

Waste not, want not

How much do you spend on groceries per week? In this chapter, I'm going to share the big savings to be made in your weekly shop – and that's good news for both you and the environment.

When I conduct courses or work with people one-on-one for coaching, I often start by discussing the weekly food spend. Though there are bigger savings to be made by negotiating a lower interest rate on your home loan or getting better deals on your insurance, these are often one-offs (or at least rare). Food, on the other hand, is something we buy every week and eat every day.

To my mind, there is no better way to consistently save money than by working on your food budget (including takeaways, which I will cover separately in the next chapter). The good news is that it's super easy to start saving money on groceries right now. Furthermore, every time you save on your grocery spend, you make a conscious choice to prioritise paying off your mortgage; it's a practice that helps to embed other savings.

Buy what you need and eat what you buy

Australians are wasteful, but we aren't the most wasteful in the world; the *UNEP Food Waste Index Report 2021* lists Australia as the tenth most wasteful country in the world. Still, 20 per cent of all groceries purchased in Australia is wasted. That amounts to one in five bags of groceries being thrown into the bin, costing the average household between $2000 and $2500 each year. So, there's $2500 right there to pay down your mortgage – and save landfill and composting!

The key to not wasting food is to buy only what you will eat and eat what you buy. Sometimes that means making do with what's in the fridge, pantry or freezer rather than rushing out to buy new ingredients every time you cook. So, let's start with checking what food you have already. We're all busy, and I know it can be hard to keep track of what is in the fridge. I'm not perfect, although I hate it when I throw out food, and the following exercise helps me keep my focus and not be wasteful.

I want you to go to your fridge. What is lurking in there? Be honest with yourself. Are you going to eat everything in your fridge before it goes off? What do you need to focus on first? If you have space, consider having a separate shelf or container for those items that you need to use up as a priority. Alternatively, you could put a sticker on those items or sign up for some 'use it up' tape produced by OzHarvest.

Are there items in your fridge that you could freeze? Bread freezes well, as does cheese. Many vegetables freeze well, especially if you freeze them first in a single layer and then transfer them to a freezer bag or container. Do you have jams or condiments that you've forgotten about? Are they still okay? If so, when are you going to eat them? And finally, give your fridge a good clean out. Reorganise things and, if necessary, put them into new containers. I find that clear containers, including jars, work best as I can see what's in them. You can do a similar exercise for your freezer. I'm a bit of a hoarder, so I often find a lot of unexpected things when I look for UFOs (unidentified frozen objects).

Don't forget the pantry and kitchen cupboards. I tend to find I have a lot of random items: right now, that's four bottles of balsamic vinegar, three bottles of Worchester sauce, two jars of paprika and two bottles of sesame oil. Once I've taken stock of my excess non-perishables, I either pass them on through my local Buy Nothing Project group (you can find one for your area on Facebook) or make a plan to use them up.

My mum likes to say that you work hard for your money, so why throw it away? She was an expert in what she called 'improvisation', meaning if she didn't have the exact ingredient called for in a recipe, she would just use something else. These days, with the help of the internet, it's easy to search for substitutes. It's even possible to cook a cake without an egg once you know how. (Hint: in many recipes, you can use a tablespoon of vinegar or soy flour.)

The purpose of this exercise is to give you a clear idea of what you have, what you tend to have too much of and what you're wasting. With this knowledge, you can use up what's been hanging around in your cupboard and fridge, and also make better choices about what to buy – and what not to buy – next time you're at the shops.

Start planning meals and making shopping lists

Whenever we set foot in a supermarket, we are likely to spend more than we planned to. Supermarkets are designed to encourage us to spend. They give us large trolleys to fill up and lots of appealing displays, including end-of-aisle specials, to tempt us. They even have chocolate bars and other temptations at the check out to get us on the way out. They lure us in with the promise of fresh produce, which is why fruit and vegetables are usually at the entrance, then make us walk through most of the store to find essential items like milk and eggs. How often have you gone into a supermarket to buy milk or bread, only to come out with ten items – and not the milk and bread? It's a thing! For foodies like me who like to cook, it's so easy to get distracted. I keep thinking of interesting things I could cook, especially with fresh produce, forgetting that there is only so much you can eat in a week.

To combat supermarket distractions, you need a plan of attack. That plan is called a shopping list. My family keeps our shopping list and a pencil attached to the fridge. Whenever we run low on something, we write it on the list. When we go shopping, we take the list with us and work through it to ensure we have purchased everything we need. It also stops us from adding additional items – unnecessary expenses – to the trolley. Pretty simple, but I'm always amazed by the number of people I see just browsing the aisles.

Also on the fridge is a larger magnetic whiteboard on which I write what we plan to eat that week. I'm not that organised, so sometimes I forget to keep it up to date, or I rewrite things. However, when I remember to write out the menu and record it on the shopping list, it is transformative. By being organised, I ensure that I have the ingredients I need to cook meals for the week. This means I'm prepared for the week and helps reduce unnecessary trips to the supermarket. If there's something I need, or something I use up when cooking a meal, I immediately add it to the shopping list.

Patricia Falcetta, the Family Joy Expert, specialises in working with neurodiverse children and their families. She is big on meal planning and calculates that she saves around $50 a week by being organised. Like me, she has a chart on the fridge that she uses to list the week's menu. Patricia says that not only does she save money, but it also helps her family navigate uncertainty: she says that many neurodiverse children need routine and predictability, and a meal plan helps with that.

'There will be certain meals that they don't like,' she said. 'But at least they know that meal is coming up, and they can prepare themselves for it.'

Patricia said that with older children, a meal plan means that if a meal comes up that they know they aren't going to like, they can choose to prepare an alternative.

Mine is not a neurodiverse family, but I do find that everything is smoother when I am organised enough to do the menu for the week. My kids notice what is for dinner (and yes, if they know they won't like something, they might make themselves some instant noodles or have some toast in the afternoon). There are no annoying 'What's for dinner?' questions, and they don't complain about what's on their plates.

Neil notices as well. Sometimes, if I get home a little later, he'll have already started preparing what is on the meal plan. (I'm blessed that we work together on household chores, but generally I choose to do most of the cooking.) Having someone who has dinner prepared – and who is using up the ingredients bought for making dinner that night – is a blessing.

Think about where you shop – it makes a difference

If you think all supermarkets are the same, think again. I've tracked prices for years. I'm frugal, so I remember the costs for key staples. My husband and I mostly shop at two places: ALDI and Costco. Occasionally we will shop at a fruit and vegetable market, and at independent grocers. I put a lot of our savings on groceries down to where we shop.

This stands up to scrutiny, too. Choice regularly surveys supermarkets, comparing the cost of a basket of items. In the Choice 2021 supermarket grocery prices survey, ALDI topped the list (as it often does) for having the cheapest basket of items. On average, the basket of items costs $80.75 at ALDI, $141.83 at Woolworths and $145.23 at Coles. That's a saving of $61.08 – almost but not quite half – on the same or similar items just by choosing a different supermarket. So, just by changing your shopping habits to buy more of your groceries at ALDI, you could pay $60 a week off your mortgage – that's $3120 each year. Interestingly, the Choice survey found that the basket of groceries purchased at IGA was similar in price, at $142.79, to the big supermarkets.

A notable omission from the Choice survey is Costco. I regularly shop at Costco for key items that are both cheap and high quality, such as beef and pork mince, bulk flour, UHT milk, toilet paper, rotisserie chickens and large tubs of vegemite (not to mention non-grocery items such as fuel and tyres, and even visits to the optometrist – all of which can offer great value). I just have to be careful to avoid purchasing 'wants', such as brandy in large dragon-shaped bottles, giant teddy bears, massage chairs and diamond rings with $500,000 price tags.

And did you know that Costco provides a lifetime warranty on appliances, as long as you maintain a current membership? If the item is no longer stocked, they'll even provide a full refund. Of course, membership isn't free, so it's important to decide (based on your proximity to a store and whether the stock suits your needs) whether it's the best value for money for you. Keep in mind, too, that you can save $5 a year on your membership if you have an Australian Business Number (ABN). It's free to apply for an ABN online, and it's probably a good idea to have one if you plan to create a side hustle (more on those in chapter 13). Currently, a Costco Gold Star Membership costs $60, while a Business Membership, which includes free business advertising on Costco's Warehouse Business Board, costs $55.

Set yourself a $100 challenge

For the last eight months my family of four has had a grocery budget of $100 a week. It's a challenge, but we consistently have change left over.

According to a 2021 report by the ABS, the average family of four spends $242 on groceries (excluding alcohol) a week. Food prices have increased in the years since, so that's likely to be a little higher now – let's round up to $250. It's also unclear if this includes cleaning items and toiletries, something that many families also spend a lot of money on. So, if $250 is the average food budget for a family of four, why would I set myself a $100 challenge? A big part of it was to reduce food waste and to force me to get rid of random things I have in my cupboard, freezer and fridge. I also saw it as a way to save money for an expensive family cruise I was planning. Over the four months leading up to our cruise, I estimate I saved around $3200. Plus, I created freezer space that I used when we went away to further reduce waste. After we returned, I decided to keep going as we already had a system and momentum was on our side. I also felt that the practice ensured we reduced waste.

Earlier in this chapter I discussed meal planning and shopping lists; setting a grocery limit is the third prong of an effective strategy to save on groceries, and it's the part that works best for my family because it prevents us from buying too much in the first place. It's important for me to point out that my kids aren't deprived when we stick to our budget of $100 a week, and neither am I. The biggest change is probably that we all eat less junk food, although our trolley does still include chocolate, biscuits, ice cream and chips. When on this challenge, I am conscious of focusing on essential items, so

I consider junk food a treat rather than an everyday item (which is pretty much how I believe it should be treated anyway).

Here are a few tips and observations for you to consider if you set yourself this challenge:

- **Have a cash kitty for groceries.** Though I could be more organised and set up a separate account for groceries, I find that cash really helps me focus. The kitty goes up and down depending on the weekly spend, and I like to maintain a buffer by collecting what's left over at the end of each week. As a result, I currently have around $160 in the kitty.

- **Go hard early.** When you start the challenge, focus on using up whatever you have at home first. I can usually spend less than $100 a week to begin with. That money then stays in reserve, building up in the kitty for when I need it.

- **Buy in bulk.** Once you have reserves in the kitty, you can use the money for investing in bigger items. For example, I use these reserves to purchase essentials in bulk, such as a 12.5 kilogram bag of flour at Costco, milk powder and other similar supplies.

- **Get creative.** Being on a challenge is a great way to use up items in your cupboard that you wouldn't usually incorporate in your cooking – and sometimes you have to get creative. Currently, I'm seeking ways of putting to use some gifted fennel powder, tins of diced vegetables, miso paste and Worcestershire sauce.

- **Discover and get rid of UFOs.** Everyone has a range of UFOs lurking in the back of their freezer. Clean them out, making use of what you can, then restock them with better-packed, labelled items.

- **Keep it on a need-to-know basis.** As I mentioned earlier, my kids aren't starving when my household is on the $100 challenge, but I still find it works best if I don't tell them about it. I also spend less on grocery shopping when I go without my kids, as whenever I take them shopping we seem to end up with what Neil and I call 'the tax' in the form of unhealthy – and unnecessary – food.

I treat my $100 budget as a challenge, but I want to recognise that for some people it's a necessity. So many people suffer from food insecurity in silence. If that's you or someone you know, while these tips can help, make sure to contact OzHarvest or your local food pantry for additional help and support. It takes courage to ask for help. Know that you can pay it forward when you are in a better position.

Eat with the seasons

I had a part-time job at Harris Farm Markets when I was a teenager. Being at work at 6 a.m. on cold winter mornings (it was Brisbane, but it was still cold for me then) and coming home with fingernails filled with dirt from bagging carrots wasn't glamorous. However, it was a great way to earn money, and it instilled in me a lifelong appreciation for quality produce and in-season eating.

These days, many items are available year-round. Supply chain disruptions notwithstanding, we receive fresh peaches, figs, garlic and other items from around the world all year long. Advances in food storage technology also mean that items like apples are often kept for months before hitting the shelves. With all this availability, it's easy to forget that most crops have an ideal season – and that when you buy in season, it's usually much cheaper. People also often plan their meals based on what's in our favourite cookbooks. That isn't wrong, but it's worth being aware of what is in season first and *then* deciding what to cook. You can find out what's in season in your area online. Sydney Markets and Harris Farm Markets, for example, both have comprehensive in-season lists on their websites. Supermarkets also highlight in-season products in their catalogues, and often they will feature those produce items as loss leaders (meaning they might offer mandarins or apples at reduced prices when they're in season to get you through the door). ALDI's Weekly Super Savers provide some of the cheapest fruit and vegetable prices I have found.

Don't forget that not all food has to come from a supermarket or local grocer. Local and car-boot markets often have a range of items sold by people who grow things as a hobby in their backyards. Many fruit and vegetable markets only open a few days a week and sell off items at reduced prices on Sunday afternoons. You will need to sharpen your elbows and get in quickly, as some people literally fight over the specials. You can also grow your own food or make friends with people who do. Even on my shady balcony, I manage to grow parsley, rocket and more. When I lived in a house in a suburban area, my neighbours would regularly give me homegrown items, and I would give them things in return. My good friend Trish regularly gives me zucchinis or oregano when I visit. If you start sharing excess food items with people, you might be surprised by what they give you in return. If you have too many homegrown items to use or give away, don't forget the joys of preserving. Mia Swainson – environmental campaigner, author of *Happy Planet Living* and another good friend – is famous for her beautiful jams made from homegrown produce. You'd be surprised by what you can preserve and how much enjoyment you'll get from cracking open those jars later – not to mention the savings.

Make your own

Finally, making your own bread, yoghurt and jams can bring extra savings that really add up. Cooking in bulk when key ingredients are cheap and freezing for future meals also makes good sense. Check out some of the super simple frugalista recipes I've put together on my website, joyfulfrugalista.com, and see what you can incorporate into your practice. You never know – it might even be fun.

Summary

- Around one in five bags of food groceries is wasted in Australia. Just by reducing food waste, you could save between $2000 and $2500 a year.

- Using meal plans and writing shopping lists will help reduce trips to the supermarket and ensure you buy only what you need.

- ALDI and Costco are generally cheaper than Coles or Woolworths. Some independent grocers can also offer good value.

- Setting yourself a challenge of living on a set amount for groceries, such as $100 a week, can help reduce waste and encourage creativity.

- Eating food that's in season will help reduce food costs and also ensure you have better-quality produce.

- Cooking your own food items from scratch rather than buying ready-made will save you a fortune.

With some discipline and creativity, most families of four could save up to $150 a week ($7800 a year) on grocery shopping. Putting that additional $150 a week onto the typical $600,000 mortgage in addition to making the standard 30-year loan payments would result in paying off that mortgage nine years and four months ahead of schedule, with a saving of $251,513 in interest over the course of the loan.

Potential savings:

Per week	$150
Per year	$7800
Time saved on your mortgage	9 years and 4 months
Interest saved on your mortgage	$251,513

And that's just from your weekly grocery bill! Next we'll look at the savings to be made on takeaway and fast food, transport, subscriptions and, of course, coffee.

Chapter 8

Taking out takeaway

It's the end of the week and you're in TGIF mode. You want to relax, and you don't feel like cooking. So, you order takeaway. There's nothing wrong with that, except it's a habit that can cost you big time – especially if it's something you do every week.

As a nation, we love good food, and we love to go out to eat and treat ourselves with takeaway food. My family lives in an apartment complex, and we're amazed and dismayed by the amount of packaging from takeaways (including delivery services) that we see lying around. We wonder how our neighbours, many of whom are young renters, can afford to eat takeaway so often. We're also concerned about the environmental impact of so much single-use packaging.

According to a survey conducted by the ABS in 2019–20, the average Australian household's weekly takeaway and fast food expenditure was $38.10. Despite economic difficulties and the soaring cost of living, Australia's love affair with buying food is going strong. While there was a sharp dip in spending on cafes, restaurants and takeaway food services during the March 2020 lockdown it has more than rebounded since then. In February 2020, for instance, Australians spent almost $4 billion on those services, but in February 2023 we spent over $5.2 billion. In recent years, app-based food delivery has made it even easier to order food to our doorsteps. Even with cost-of-living pressures, Australians continue to rely on takeaway food, making around 7000 orders an hour through Uber Eats, Menulog and other delivery providers, which comes to $2.6 billion on food and drink in a year. In its most recent survey at the time of writing, Canstar calculates that Australians spend $60 a week (that's $260 a month and $3120 a year) on food delivery services, which is almost double what was estimated in 2022.

Clearly, getting takeaway or eating out every week adds up. In this chapter, I am going to show you ways that you can reduce your reliance on takeaway and fast food, make some major savings and still enjoy the occasional meal out – at a discount.

Reducing – or cutting out – the takeaway toll

As post-COVID, inflation-affected statistics about household spending on takeaway aren't yet available (at the time of writing), for the purpose of this chapter I'm going base my calculations on the 2019–20 ABS figure I mentioned earlier, rounding up slightly to $40 a week for simplicity. As is reflected in those more recent estimates of $60 a week, many people I know spend more than this – especially if there are kids involved. Even a single McDonalds trip for a family of four can cost close to $50 if you include individual preferences rather than going with a family pack.

Though $40 a week doesn't sound like much, cutting out takeaway and fast food altogether would save the average household $2080 a year. Paid directly into the typical mortgage, that shaves over two years off the mortgage and saves almost $60,000 in interest.

Potential savings:

Per week	$40
Per year	$2080
Time saved on your mortgage	2 years and 2 months
Interest saved on your mortgage	$59,846

It can be difficult to cut takeaway out entirely, particularly if your household is busy, but using these strategies can set you on the path to real savings.

Adopt an attitude of gratitude

Most nights, before my family and I share dinner, we say grace. It might seem old-fashioned, but I believe it's important for us as we come together as a family. We made it a habit when my friend Leilani came to stay with us for an extended period. Leilani is a proud Torres Strait Islander woman, and her faith is important to her. Saying grace was non-negotiable when Leilani was with us, and I loved how my kids got into the practice. What it taught them was the importance of having an attitude of gratitude.

Mealtimes are important in Leilani's culture.

'For First Nations people, it is more than just the food or the dollar value,' she said. 'It is our ability to come together and reconnect, which is consistent with our cultural values of family first. We sit around the table, and then we say, "Right, so what's been going on?"'

For my family, sharing a meal has a similar meaning. It's not about critiquing it or ensuring it is restaurant standard but being thankful we have each other, a roof over our heads and a meal on the table. In these difficult times, these are luxuries that not everyone has.

Australia is lucky to enjoy a melting pot of cuisines. We have some of the best food in the world, and we love dining out and cooking amazing food. It can therefore be easy to overlook the joys of simple home-style cooking.

Home-cooked meals aren't the same as their restaurant counterparts. They typically contain less salt and fat, and they often look a little different each time because they don't have to be plated and replicated with commercial consistency. It's okay for home-cooked meals to be basic. It's okay to have a simple bowl of potato and leek soup, a quiche with uneven edges or just cheese on toast. It's okay if your homemade cottage pie isn't Instagrammable. Adopting an attitude of gratitude towards our food, however, is transformative. How lucky are we, at a time when OzHarvest estimates that over two million households a year experience food insecurity, to share a meal? How lucky are we to be together?

Many years ago, I went on a Buddhist retreat in the foothills of the Snowy Mountains. It was very basic vegetarian fare, but after a few days I began to savour it differently. I was eating with more of my senses and it tasted delicious. The key difference was taking the time to be mindful about what I was eating and to have that sense of gratitude. I'm talking about gratitude because it affects our takeaway food culture. We tend to think something made by a professional will be more exciting or taste better, but by the time it gets to the dining room table it's often disappointing. By deprioritising restaurant meals and focusing instead on enjoying the simple things at home, you can save a fortune.

Cook in batches

Many of us lead busy lives, and being too busy – or too tired – to cook is a typical reason for ordering takeaway. You can pre-empt this, however, by ensuring you always have something in the freezer by batch cooking.

Simply pick a day, or a half day, every month or so and have a big cook up. You can even make it social if you want and invite other people over. The important thing, however, is to cook dishes that you can freeze and have ready for when you need them. Here's a super frugal tip: save empty butter containers and use them to store your batch cooking. They're the perfect size for single-portion meals, and they stack well. Best of all, they're free! No need to go out and buy something expensive as part of a new organisational routine.

How you use the spoils of your batch cooking is up to you. Some people are super organised and like to ensure meals for every night of the week are prepped and ready in the freezer. I prefer to cook from scratch most nights, but I rely on the freezer those nights when I am feeling too tired to cook.

My husband's niece Ashleigh is a big fan of batch cooking. She previously worked as a teacher and had long nights at school or with other pursuits such as dancing. She would regularly set up a time when she would make a big batch of favourite meals such as curries, divide them into portions and then freeze them. She would then pull out these meals once or twice a week. It was much cheaper than takeaway – and quicker, too. All up she saves over $50 a week by batch cooking instead of grabbing some takeaway on the way home.

When doing some batch cooking, it can be a good idea to label items to ensure they are easy to find – especially if you're using up those butter containers. I find that non-permanent markers or stickers are often good for labelling food items. I also like to use clear plastic containers or glass jars because it's easier to see what the items are.

Have some simple go-to meals

When you know how, it's often quicker and easier to make a simple meal or snack at home than it is order takeaway.

Glenda Stevens is a successful CEO of a not-for-profit organisation, but for many years she was a struggling single mother of three children. She put herself through university and sent her children to private schools while slashing ten years off the mortgage on her Sydney home through adopting simple living strategies.

'Rather than takeaways,' she said, 'I would make scrambled eggs at home.'

Low on time and with three hungry mouths to feed, Glenda made quick and easy go-to meals – and it looks like it worked.

By 'go-to' meals, I mean simple meals that you can make on autopilot. Often, deciding what to have for dinner is part of the mental load. If you have a few meals that you know you can cook quickly, easily and with ingredients you keep on standby, you're halfway there. Here are some of my favourites:

- **Toasties.** With a sandwich press, some cheese and a bit of ham, chicken or tomato, you can make a meal in minutes.
- **Instant noodles.** My family serves instant noodles with a can of tuna on top for protein and flavour, and I like to add frozen broccoli to the boiling water, and fish balls if I have them. My friend KC likes to make hers with kimchi and cracks an egg on top to poach as the noodles cook.
- **Spaghetti with pesto.** Both ingredients can be stored in the cupboard until they're needed, and you can add protein in the form of chicken, prawns or chickpeas if you have any on hand – or just keep it simple.
- **Omelettes.** I love my cast iron omelette pan (purchased at a tip shop years ago). It makes the best omelettes, especially when I include herbs from my balcony.

If you know there's no way you'll find the energy to cook even the simplest meal from scratch when you're tired or busy (and batch cooking isn't your style), consider investing in a few easy-to-prepare pre-made items when you go shopping. My favourite is Chinese dumplings (jiaozi) and I'm also partial to spanakopita, while Neil likes crumbed fish and potato gems. These sorts of meals can be your last line of defence against ordering takeaway, so it's good to have them on hand for when you need them.

Start a new ritual – fridge Fridays and pizza nights

Many Australian households enjoy takeaway on Friday nights and then spend Saturday morning throwing out food to fit the next grocery shop into the fridge and pantry. Before you go shopping for more food, why not have a clean out? Having a Fridge Friday ritual of using up leftovers in creative ways is a great way to avoid the takeaway trap and cut down on food waste.

Fridge Fridays can be as simple as just eating what you have, finishing up leftover meals or putting together an improvised (and thoroughly non-traditional) antipasti plate with the bits and pieces rolling around in the bottom of the fridge. If you have more energy, you could incorporate leftover ingredients or even meals into fresh dishes, such as fried rice, stir-fry, pasta or soup.

Friday night is also pizza night in my household. We had so much fun making pizza from scratch at another family's home for their Friday pizza night that we decided to make it a regular thing at our own. As an extension of fridge Friday, as I also use it as an opportunity to use up leftovers. That is, I will usually make one pizza that is super creative with unusual leftovers and unexpected vegetables, while my boys still prefer the standard salami, ham and mozzarella toppings.

My sons look forward to pizza night so much, and I hear them telling their friends about it with excitement on Fridays. Recently, they had a few mates over for pizza night, and they all took turns to roll out their own dough and choose their own toppings. Here is the dough recipe we use.

Friday pizza night dough

Ingredients:

- 200ml water
- 1 tablespoon olive oil
- 1 teaspoon salt
- 1¾ teaspoons yeast
- 2½ cups plain or baker's flour

Method:

1. Mix all ingredients in a bread maker on a dough setting until smooth and elastic. Alternatively, mix it in a thermacooker or food processor, or go old-school and knead it by hand.
2. Place the dough in a large bowl, cover with clingwrap or a damp towel and allow the mixture to rise for around 45 minutes.
3. Roll the dough out thinly on a floured board into circles. You can throw it in the air of you want, or you could just use a rolling pin.
4. Place the rolled out dough on a floured pizza tray and top with tomato paste (or Italian tomato sauce) and toppings of choice.
5. Bake in the oven at around 220° degrees for ten minutes or until crispy.

If we decided to order in, we would probably be paying between $20 and $25 each for comparable gourmet pizzas. Most Friday nights I make four (a double batch of pizza dough, with each batch making two). This makes more than we need, which means we have leftover pizza on hand for snacks over the weekend. Even allowing for the cost of ingredients, by making our own pizzas rather than ordering in gourmet takeaway we make a saving of around $100.

BYO work lunch

I used to have a job in a workplace with the best cafe. Every day they had a mix of seasonal specials. Friday was often laksa day, plus they made super fresh salads and Asian-inspired dishes. Most of my colleagues ate at the cafe regularly. But not me. I'm the queen of BYO lunches. It's a habit that has saved me tens of thousands of dollars over the years.

I don't mind 'boring' lunchboxes because I know they have helped me – and continue to help me – achieve my financial goals. Sometimes I choose to buy my lunch because I've forgotten to bring something with me or because I have a lunch date with someone. On these occasions I use my gold card (which I'll discuss in chapter 11). I don't mind sushi, a kebab or banh mi for lunch, but they are an occasional treat rather than an everyday item.

It can cost between $10 and $20 to buy your lunch. By the time you include a drink, the average spend is usually on the higher side, but for the sake of convenience I'll use $15 as an average bought-lunch price. On the other hand, it usually costs between $2.50 and $5 to make your lunch, depending on whether you are eating leftovers or making something from scratch. Assuming you spend $5, you would *save* $10 every time you bring your lunch in from home rather than buying it. If you were to do this every single business day, you could save $220 a month, which comes up to $2400 a year. As you probably don't work five days a week for all 52 weeks of the year, I've assumed 48 weeks in a year.

Potential savings:

Per week	$50
Per year	$2400
Time saved on your mortgage	1 year and 1 month
Interest saved on your mortgage	$30,517

Socialising done smart

'Let's catch up for dinner!'

We've all been in situations where someone suggests a group catch-up. Maybe it's a boys' (or ladies') night out, a family get-together or dinner and drinks with friends. It can be hard to say no without it seeming like you're being, well, mean and Scroogey. If you have a gold card (to be discussed in chapter 11), you will likely have funds set aside for a bit of fun out. But if you haven't – or don't want to use it – it can be hard. I'm passionate about creating events that are, when possible, financially inclusive. You never know who might be struggling with their money, so it's best not to put anyone in a situation where they have to spend money they mightn't have so they can see you.

Invite friends over

Catching up with people who are important to us doesn't have to be expensive. I recently had friends over for pizza Friday. We had fun making tailored pizzas, and after dinner we sat around the firepit with some port. It didn't cost us – or them – a lot of money, and we got to chat and chat and chat. The dishes and clean-up are unavoidable, but a nice thing about entertaining at home is that you don't have to worry about the kitchen closing or being hurried on for the next sitting. With good friends who accept you as you are, meals at home – from pizza to potluck – can be a lot of fun.

Be clever about where you go

There are times when you don't want to entertain at home. For instance, you might not want to invite someone over to your place on a first date, nor are you likely to want to bring professional contacts or large groups of people you don't really know into your home. So, you go to a venue. The problem is the inevitable argument over bill splitting, particularly when you have big drinkers or people with fine tastes in your party. Even worse, I've heard of instances of the person who collects all the cash on behalf of others in the group pocketing any leftovers! One way of avoiding this altogether is by picking a club or pub. People can order and pay for what they like, including drinks. We find this avoids a lot of problems or issues, and an added bonus is that it is often good value.

Though I might sound like a cheapskate, in truth Neil and I like to take other people out reasonably regularly. This reflects our spirit of hospitality, and it is just something we like to do now that we're in a good financial situation. However, it's important to look after yourself first – and that means focusing on your goal of paying off your mortgage.

Use vouchers and apps to get a good deal

Would you, could you, go out with a friend or on a date with someone who uses a discount voucher? I would.

There are now more ways to eat out cheaply than ever before. A popular group buying platform that offers discounts and deals is Groupon. I've had some terrific Groupon meals over the years and found it's a great way to try different places. Groupon isn't the only group buying platform, and websites such as Scoopon and LivingSocial offer discounts of up to 50 per cent. In practice, however, the discount is rarely that big, and I find that many of these sites are more useful in bigger cities where there is more choice, but you may be surprised at what's offered. You never know unless you check it out. Best of all, many of these sites have apps, making them handy for searching when you are out and about, including when you're on holiday.

If you're flexible with your dining, you could sign up to EatClub (which also has an app). EatClub connects potential diners with restaurants that have empty tables. It's essentially a last-minute reservation system where you can get discounted meals. You can even use geolocation to find offers within 2 km. It's a good resource for when you meet up with friends and then decide to go to dinner, or if you're new to an area.

The early bird catches the worm, and early diners can get great discounts. If you plan to eat out early, such as before going to the movies or the theatre, then consider using a site such as FirstTable. FirstTable offers a half-price discount to patrons who are prepared to turn up early. There are a few restrictions – turning up on time rather than casually sauntering in at a normal dining time being one of them. The dine-early deal also only covers food, not drinks, so make sure you are aware of that before ordering a second cocktail. FirstTable can also be an option for lunch discounts on less busy days.

Summary

- Australians spend billions every year on takeaway, fast food, and cafe and restaurant meals, with many people choosing these options every week. Reducing this spend is a terrific way to free up more money for your mortgage.

- Cultivate gratitude with your food and enjoy the simple delights of home cooking.

- Cook up food in batches and freeze for when life is busy or difficult.

- Have a few simple go-to dishes that you can prepare in a hurry without much time or energy.

- Celebrate the end of the week with a new at-home ritual rather than getting takeaway or dining out. Fridge Friday is a great way to enjoy leftovers (ahead of the weekend grocery shop), and making pizza at home can be a fun activity for the whole household.

- There is no such thing as a boring homemade lunchbox. It's fuel for mortgage-paying champions.
- Choose financially inclusive venues for catching up with other people for a meal, such as pubs and clubs, where people pay for their own food and drink.
- Group buying platforms and discount apps make it easy to get a discount on dining out.

As you can see, there are plenty of ways to avoid the takeaway trap (and even make the occasional night out more affordable) – and they can be just as hassle free, and sometimes more fun, than ordering in. In the next chapter I'm going to help you to reduce your transport costs.

Chapter 9

Transport rethink

Before COVID, for many of us the working day looked like this: get up early, shower, get dressed, have a cup of coffee, get in the car and drive to work, buy another cup of coffee, work, buy lunch, work, buy another cup of coffee and a snack to get through the mid-afternoon slump, get in the car and drive home. The pandemic forced many of us to rethink how we work and live. If you were able to work from home, were you surprised by how much you saved? Notwithstanding tax deductions and the additional energy costs of working from home, most people saved more than they might have otherwise expected because they didn't have to pay for transport.

We've seen another trend in recent years of people, especially first home buyers, buying in suburbs further out from the CBD or in regional towns or centres. During the lockdowns, many of us experienced how unpleasant being confined in small spaces can be, so many chose to buy homes away from densely populated urban centres in favour of roomier houses and access to outdoor space. Others made the change purely because that's what they were able to afford. Then, as many of us were working from home for long periods, we kind of forgot about how expensive petrol can be – that is, until petrol prices started going up just as we headed back to the office. Combined with growing mortgage repayments due to rising interest rates, rising petrol costs caught many people unaware.

Higher petrol costs are leading people to re-examine their lifestyles and approaches to transport. In this chapter, I'm going to dig into exactly how much it costs to run a car and look at ways that you can save money on transport.

Adding up the costs of running a car

According to the 2021 census there are 1.8 vehicles per Australian household, with 91 per cent of households reporting having at least one vehicle. The total cost of having and running a car will be different for everyone. It depends on the make and model of your car, where you live, how you use your car and plenty of other factors.

Forget about the cost of petrol for now; let's start by looking at how much it costs just to *have* a car. For illustrative purposes, I've based my calculations on the cost of running a Ford Territory, my family car, in the ACT. I've also assumed a car loan of $20,000 at 7.5 per cent over seven years, though many people choose a finance package offered by their car dealership, which tends to cost more. We don't have a car loan ourselves, but I know many people do.

Table 4: The basic costs of running a car

Item	Cost per year
Registration	$582.90
Compulsory third party insurance	$419.10
Comprehensive insurance	$1583.66
ACT registration road rescue fee	$28.40

Item	Cost per year
Road safety contribution	$2.50
Motor accident levy for passenger vehicle	$16.00
Registration lifetime care and support levy for passenger vehicle	$45.70
Servicing and repairs	$2000
Roadside assistance	$214
Tyres	$600
Car loan repayments	$3684
Total	**$9176.26**

As set out in table 4, factoring in only the most basic costs – insurance, registration, upkeep and so on – it takes $176.46 a week, or a little over $9000 a year, to run a Ford Territory in the ACT. In table 5 I estimate how much it costs to drive that car (based on an average commute – 20 km each workday and a bit more on the weekend).

Table 5: The basic costs of driving a car

Item	Cost per year
Petrol	$2600
Parking at work (48 weeks/year)	$3600
Toll roads (48 weeks/year)	$1920
Car washes	$100
Accident excess	Nil (hopefully)
Total	**$8220**

This comes out to a further $158 a week, $8220 a year (assuming you don't pay for parking and tolls on holidays), meaning that the total cost of running this car as a typical commuter comes up to $335 a week – $17,340 a year.

It's important to know how much it costs you to use your car, as this can help you decide how many cars you need or want, or even if you need a car at all. Sometimes buying closer to work might be cheaper than commuting in. That said, if you work in an area where real estate is expensive it might not be feasible to buy nearby.

Choose your car according to your needs

Neil and I each had a car when we met. I had a 17-year-old Toyota RAV4 that was still going strong, and Neil had a dual cab Isuzu D-MAX. When Neil moved in, however, we decided that we didn't need two cars, so I gave mine to my dad (who still drives it around Melbourne), Neil sold his D-MAX (I couldn't drive it) and we purchased a near-new Ford Territory. We paid for it in full by withdrawing funds from our mortgage and then made extra repayments to pay the mortgage down quickly.

Before purchasing our car, we sat down and worked out our needs. With two young children with various sporting commitments and other appointments, and family living in a rural area, it was clear that we still needed a vehicle. We also wanted something that could tow and was suitable for driving on unsealed roads. As we love skiing, we wanted our car to be safe for long road trips, including in icy conditions, but it also needed to be easy to drive (especially for me), comfortable for the whole family and, crucially, easy to park in the apartment carpark.

I'm mentioning all of this because so often people don't think about what they need in a car before they buy. A car is often more than just a means of transport; it can represent freedom, independence and the driver's personality. Accordingly, many people invest heavily in a car (especially a first car) without thinking through whether the car is truly suitable for their needs – or considering the financial consequences. Is a sports car the most suitable if you're planning to have a family, for instance? Or what about a large SUV if you have a tiny garage? Do you really need to buy new? Is it smart to get an EV if your apartment building doesn't have a charging station? And, as I mentioned in chapter 6, don't forget what your choice can mean for insurance premiums. It sounds obvious, but thinking about and articulating your specific needs, then choosing a car that meets those needs, is an essential part of bringing down the cost of ownership.

New or used?

Have you ever seen photos or videos on social media of people getting a new car with a big red bow on it? It's a happy moment for them, and the feeling of driving away in a brand-new car with that new car smell is special. I'm always pleased for friends and family members when they announce their exciting new purchase, and I say suitably congratulatory things, but I'm often a little worried. I'm conscious that, despite the thrill of the purchase, this financial decision might end up costing them a lot of money in the long run. In my experience, they are often signing themselves up to years of debt for a depreciating asset.

The moment you drive your new car out of a car dealership, it begins to depreciate. At least, it does in normal times: supply chain issues temporarily altered that, but it will likely revert to depreciating rapidly again.

In contrast, you can often find good value buying a second-hand vehicle, especially it's been driven by a single owner for only a few years. If it has been maintained, has a good service history and is still under manufacturer's warranty you might be able to score a bargain. That's what we did. We purchased a three-year old Ford Territory second hand by online auction through Pickles. It had been used as a government vehicle, had only 37,000 km on the clock and was in excellent condition. We purchased it for $17,000; then, by the time we paid for it to be transported to Canberra, registered and amended slightly it cost us $19,500. Its insurance value was $24,000, and a comparable brand-new car would have cost around $45,000 at that time. That's a saving of $25,500.

To avoid getting caught up in the emotion of it all and ensure you prioritise your needs over your wants, spend some time doing your own research before you head out to a car dealership. Some useful cheat sheets on what to look out for when considering specific used car makes and models can be found at carsales.com.au, the NRMA website and ReDriven. It's always a good idea to take someone with you, too. Remember, don't be pressured into anything and, above all, don't buy a car before taking it for a pre-purchase inspection.

Sell the second car

Do you have a second car sitting in your garage? If so, have you considered selling it? People often keep a second car because they want to have a sense of independence. What if their significant other is away? How will they get around? However, based on my calculations in table 4, my family saves over $175 a week just by not having a second car – and that doesn't include things like petrol or parking. That leaves plenty of money spare for taking an Uber or a taxi if we need to get somewhere while someone else is using the car. Sometimes, I take an Uber just because it's easier, such as when going to an unfamiliar place for an appointment or interview. I never drive to a job interview, for instance. The last thing I need is the stress of driving and parking! I also give myself permission to Uber home from events where there is alcohol. It's liberating to know that we have extra money set aside to allow ourselves to do that.

Shane, who I know in a professional context, is someone I've had a random conversation with about the benefits of frugal lifestyle who listened. One lunchtime, when I was foraging for cherry plums in our office complex (while wearing a suit, as you do) to make jam with, we started talking about saving money. That discussion, I later learned, led to Shane and his wife ditching their second car.

It turns out that getting rid of a car they weren't using that much and using rideshares on the occasions when a second car would have been handy – which Shane says, after five or so years, has been about three times – made much more financial sense for them.

In normal times, people usually make a loss when they sell their second car – especially if they bought it new. This is because new cars depreciate quickly. Luxury cars such as BMWs have been known to depreciate by as much as $20,000 in the first year, for example. However, since early 2020, it's become a little harder to predict. Supply chain issues, notably a shortage in semiconductor chips and disruptions in shipping freight, have resulted in a chronic shortage of passenger vehicles in Australia, which has pushed the price of vehicles up. I have friends who have made a profit when selling their second-hand car. So, sell that car, take the profit and whack that money straight onto your mortgage to bring the principal down.

It's difficult to estimate potential savings here, but I'll illustrate the impact of this choice using our Ford Territory as an example again. If we were to sell our Ford Territory, we'd probably get around $20,000 and then save $335 a week ($17,340 a year) in running costs. Paid straight into a $600,000 mortgage, that $20,000 would result in a $23,168 saving on interest and reduce repayments by $120 per month. Increasing mortgage repayments by the $335 a week saved on running costs, however, the mortgage would be repaid seven years and seven months ahead of the typical 30-year term, and $220,474 in interest would be saved.

Save on petrol

The tank is almost empty. Your fortnightly pay hits your account, but it's right before a long weekend and, before you can fill up, prices at the bowser soar. We've all been there. Petrol prices are notorious for changing frequently and varying between different petrol stations. Still, you can save money by being savvy when it comes to buying petrol.

Neil likes to monitor petrol prices and I'm not sure he has ever found cheaper petrol prices than at the Costco warehouse at our closest major shopping centre. If you live within an easy drive of Costco, the cost of membership (which we discussed in chapter 7) may be worth it for fuel alone.

Those of us who don't live close to a Costco or don't want to purchase a membership can save on petrol by using fuel-price apps. In states and territories other than Victoria and the ACT, service stations are required to register their fuel prices each day. Several database apps capture and display this information to make it easier for motorists to choose where to fill up. Popular apps include MotorMouth, GasBuddy, Refueler, Fuel Map and Petrol Spy. There are also three government-run apps for different jurisdictions: NSW FuelCheck, FuelWatch (Western Australia) and MyFuel NT. There's no clear frontrunner, but Choice has completed a detailed analysis of which apps work best in which state or territory that's worth checking out. Of note is the Fuel Price Lock function on the My 7-Eleven app, which lets users lock in a particular fuel price before filling up at a 7-Eleven service station.

Carpool

Carpooling was big 20 or 30 years ago, and with the high cost of petrol, a shortage of parking in inner-city areas and the desire of many to be more sustainable, it's back in a big way – particularly for commuters. Platforms and apps such as Coseats, Kapuddle, Share Your Ride and Carpool World are good ways to connect with people who want to carpool – whether you're just going into the CBD every Thursday at 8 a.m., or you need to get from Adelaide to Darwin. You could also consider reaching out through your work networks. Do you have a noticeboard at work, perhaps even online, or could you put up a poster? You might end up making new friends and broadening your social circle.

Car sharing

After I'd given my car to my dad and before Neil and I had bought the Ford Territory, there were occasions when I needed to use a car – and I couldn't drive his D-MAX (I'm too short). For those odd times when I needed access to a car for things such as shopping and appointments, and a quick Uber or a taxi ride wasn't going to cut it, I used the car-share service GoGet.

Many of us have used hire cars before, and the concept of car sharing is similar: hiring someone else's vehicle for a specified period of time. The main difference is that with a car-share service you generally hire (and pay) by the hour, typically after paying a monthly membership fee. There are four dedicated car-sharing parking spaces (called 'pods') close to where I live, so I could just reserve a car online, walk to the pod, unlock the car with my GoGet smart card, put the keys in the ignition and head off. Easy peasy. I didn't even need to worry about fuel! Best part of it – I never had to undertake maintenance or return the car to a central hire facility a long way away. I've noticed Popcar is now popular where I live too, and there are plenty of other companies that offer car sharing, including Hertz 24/7, Flexicar and GreenShareCar. Not all companies operate in all areas area, so find a company that is close to you.

According to GoGet, most cars are driven for less than an hour a day, and many people have a second car that they drive less than 8000 km a year. They calculate that someone with a second car that they drive irregularly (say, less than 3000 km a year) could save $5535.76 each year if they used a GoGet instead. There are now also several other peer-to-peer car-share platforms. When Neil and I were in the USA recently we used a site called Turo. We saved a fortune on car hire compared with what we'd have spent at a commercial company. Turo now operates in Australia, along with other companies such as Uber Carshare (formerly Car Next Door). You never know – you might have a neighbour looking to rent out their car for a short period of time. Why buy – and pay all the upkeep costs detailed in table 4 – when you can rent on demand? You could also use these platforms to rent out your car when you are not using it.

Potential savings:

Per week	$106.50
Per year	$5535.76
Time saved on your mortgage	7 years and 4 months
Interest saved on your mortgage	$201,262

Motorcycle

Ever wanted to ride a motorbike? The good news is that motorcycles are a cost-effective way of getting around.

Sonia van den Berg is on a mission to make motorcycling safer and more accessible, particularly for women. She is active in the Female Riders of Canberra (FRoC) Facebook group, and she regularly leads women in organised rides. She is also CEO of Riders Lane Canberra, a social enterprise aimed at helping people learn about motorbike maintenance. Given her love of motorcycling, I asked her to crunch some numbers about how much people could save on riding a motorbike rather than a car. The results surprised me.

Based on the comparison between a small car such as a Fiat 500 (noting many people would purchase a larger car, which would cost more to buy and run) and a Honda CB500F, you would save around $13,214 upfront and then just over $5300 a year in various running costs (including parking).

Sonia said that a bike motor is less complex and, as there are fewer parts that might need replacing, motorbikes tend to have longer lifespans. 'A 20-year-old bike is common, whereas a 20-year-old car is not,' she said.

She also noted that, overall, a motorbike has a lower initial cost outlay, slower depreciation, lower maintenance costs and slightly lower rego. Often, parking is free. Registration costs are even lower for motorcycles under 300cc.

'For people just wanting a vehicle to commute around town, a 300cc bike is adequate, whereas we don't have cars that small in Australia,' she said.

Potential savings:

Per month	$442
Per year	$5300
Time saved on your mortgage	7 years and 3 months
Interest saved on your mortgage	$195,201

Cycling

Peter Adeney, aka Mr Money Mustache, famously credits cycling wherever and whenever he can as a way of saving money. Fans around the world follow his advice, and many people in the Financial Independence, Retire Early (FIRE) community incorporate cycling as one of their frugal hacks. I was influenced by this trend when I sold my outer suburban house and moved to an inner-city apartment. I had realised that nearly all my time outside of work was being taken up commuting, leaving little to no time for exercise, and I knew I needed to incorporate health and wellbeing into my daily routine.

The move was a game changer. It allowed me to cycle to work along the shore of Lake Burley Griffin, past the National Library of Australia, the High Court of Australia and the National Gallery of Australia. While some mornings were a bit fresh, the spectacular scenery more than made up for it. Though I now typically work from home, I still get around on my bicycle a lot – including for shopping trips. I'm often amazed at how many groceries I can fit in the basket on the back of my bike. Using my bike has allowed me to go without a second car, save money on gym fees and reduce the use of my car for short trips. Based on these changes, I calculate that my $380 second-hand Giant bicycle has saved me at least $50,000 over the six years I have owned it.

Neil also cycles to work. His commute is about 5 km each way. The incidental exercise makes a big difference to his health and wellbeing, and he also saves a lot of money with no additional petrol or parking costs. One night, we went out for dinner to celebrate our anniversary, and the drive home took us past Neil's workplace. Suddenly, I had a realisation: our meal cost around about the same amount Neil would have spent on parking every week if he drove his car. In other words, the savings we were making every week by cycling instead of driving easily paid for occasional luxuries such as dining out.

It's clear how opting to cycle instead of drive can reduce your transport costs, but consider too how commuting by bike could save you money in other ways. For example, if you cycle to and from work a few days a week or more, and then walk or use your bike to get around on the weekend, do you still need your gym membership to keep fit? You might need the training support, group fitness classes or specialised equipment offered at your gym; however, depending on your goals, you may find that supplementing your daily routine of walking and cycling with a bit of body-weight exercise at home does the trick. I'll explore gym memberships in greater detail in the next chapter, but there are definitely savings to be had.

Potential savings (having sold the second car and ditched the gym membership, choosing instead to walk and cycle):

Per month	$1478
Per year	$17,736
Time saved on your mortgage	15 years
Interest saved on your mortgage	$384,981

Public transport

Taking a bus or train was not a popular choice during the pandemic. Australia's national census reported that train travel decreased from 488,012 people in 2016 to 170,326 in 2021. It's hard to take a train when you're in lockdown. However, now people are returning to the office, public transport usage is becoming more common again – due in no small part to the high cost of petrol and the focus on adopting more sustainable methods of transport.

Take a moment now to think about where you drive your car most often. Are there public transport routes you could use instead? Most states have handy apps that will get you where you need to go (many people like to use an app called Moovit), but I tend to just use Google Maps. Simply enter your destination and select the public transport icon at the top of the screen (it looks like a train) and let Google calculate the best route using public transport. You can even change where you plan to leave from and the date and time you want to leave or arrive by, which can be particularly helpful if you're planning a trip in advance. Though public transport may not always be the best option for you (particularly if you live regionally), it's definitely worth considering. If it's convenient enough for your needs, you're likely to save a lot on car upkeep, petrol and parking – and Ubers.

If you're in the market to buy a property, make sure you think about public transport. I'm always surprised by the number of people who don't. It's a crucial decision, as transport costs can have a huge impact on your overall financial situation. We live 200 metres away from a light rail station – just two stops and we're in central Canberra – and being close to public transport has been transformative for us. Though we usually prefer to walk or cycle, there are times when it is nice to have the convenience of just jumping on the light rail. We remember once going out with friends and heading home on the light rail close to midnight. It was liberating not having to worry about parking or catching a taxi or an Uber at that time of night. My eldest son sometimes takes the light rail to meet with his friends in the city. My youngest son, who's still in primary school, takes the light rail and bus several times a week to go to table tennis training. He's proud of taking himself there and I love how it's giving him independence.

So, how much can you save? That varies tremendously depending on where you live and what type of public transport is nearby. However, my friend Leilani shows that if you go entirely without a car and choose to live near where you work, you can save a fortune in transport costs (more on that in a moment). That also needs to be weighed up against the cost of housing close to public transport and where you work. While it's still generally cheaper overall to live further away from the CBD and pay a little more for public transport, there are exceptions.

Going carless

Yes, you can get by without a car – especially if you live in an urban area. Many people do!

My friend Leilani, who you may remember from chapter 8, doesn't have a car. She decided not to drive after being involved in a car accident when she was young. She doesn't even have a licence. Leilani lives within walking distance of her workplace, so she doesn't need to commute to and from work. Her apartment is five minutes by bus from a major shopping centre and around fifteen minutes from the city centre. She shops for groceries once a week and has larger items delivered. She currently spends between $25 and $30 a fortnight on public transport, reducing her spend by travelling during off-peak times when possible. She budgets $50 a fortnight for taxis, calling drivers she knows and trusts, to attend events such as lectures. Leilani is known to her taxi drivers, and they look after her well. That means Leilani typically spends up to $80 a fortnight ($40 a week) on transport. Given that someone with a car of the make and model my family owns could spend over $300 a week, Leilani is saving around $260 a week, or $13,520 a year, by choosing not to own or drive a car.

Summary

- Before getting excited about buying your dream car, wrapped in a bow, take some time to examine what you really need.

- It costs more to own and run a car than you might think. Our second-hand Ford Territory costs around $176 a week just to have it registered and sitting in the garage, and approximately $335 a week if we used it like a typical household does.

- Considering how much it costs just to have a second car, think about whether you really need it. Could you sell the second car and put the money on your mortgage?

- Pay attention to petrol prices and plan ahead. You can even use apps to shop around and lock in the best price for petrol.

- Motorcycles are cheaper than cars to buy, run and maintain. Could swapping the car for a motorcycle be a solution for you?

- Cycling is cheap, and commuting by bike can save you tens of thousands of dollars a year. You might even be able to ditch the gym membership.

- If you decide to sell the second car – or go completely carless – think about other ways you can get around for less. There are many ways you might be able to meet your transport needs, including carpooling and car sharing, walking and cycling, and taking public transport.

Changing how you get from A to B can save you thousands of dollars a year, which can translate into time off your mortgage and save you paying unnecessary interest. Even if you can't ditch the car altogether, rethinking your transport needs and adjusting your habits accordingly is likely to net you some great savings. Next I'm going to explore how you can avoid falling into subscription traps and save on entertainment at home.

Chapter 10

Subscriptions sneak up on you

In the 1990s, a Foxtel representative knocked on my husband's door.

'I'm installing in the area,' he said. 'Would you like me to arrange Foxtel for you today?'

At that time, the contract was 'only' $70 a month.

'No, thank you,' Neil replied. 'I'd rather put that money on my mortgage.'

The rep was flabbergasted, but prioritising his mortgage over more discretionary spending – such as satellite TV – was important to Neil, and both of us maintain that attitude to spending and saving even today.

Now that you've seen how even small savings can, over time, make a huge difference to how quickly you can pay your mortgage off, you can probably guess where I'm going to take you in this chapter. That's right: let's talk about entertainment subscriptions.

Satellite TV

Before YouTube or streaming, most of my friends had Foxtel (as did most of Neil's neighbours). Some people I knew even had giant discs in their backyards that enabled them to watch channels from overseas.

While streaming services have disrupted satellite TV, a surprising number of Australians still pay for it. In 2021 the Australian Communications and Media Authority assessed there were approximately 1.9 million subscribers to satellite and IPTV services such as Foxtel and Fetch TV – and it can be a hefty expense. Foxtel, for example, starts at $69 a month just for entertainment and movies, and goes up to $140 a month for the package that includes sports, Netflix and other features. $140 a month adds up to $1680 a year. Once you have signed up, you often feel obligated to keep going. But do you really need it? Is there a more frugal way to watch what you want?

There may be specific reasons why you want a particular satellite TV package. For instance, if you work in media or politics, you might like to have access to certain news programs. Or perhaps sport is your passion, and Foxtel gives you all the sport you want. In general, however, a simple money-saving hack is to move from a satellite subscription to online streaming services that meet your needs.

If you have a satellite subscription because you're a big sports fan, for example, consider switching to Kayo Sports or Stan Sport. According to Finder, for $25 a month Kayo offers a sports viewing experience beyond what's available on Foxtel. Meanwhile, a Foxtel package with sport starts at $74 a month. Stan Sport can be added onto a Stan subscription and comes out to about $25 to $36 a month in total.

Not all sports codes are covered by one subscription. It depends on broadcasting and streaming rights, which can change season to season. For example, Super Rugby is currently hosted by Stan, while Kayo has NRL and AFL. If you want to watch all of these sports, it may still work out cheaper for you to sign up to a couple of services but only for the duration of the seasons that are important to you. For instance, my husband purchases Kayo in winter to watch the NRL and then cancels it during the finals as they're streamed free on 9Now.

As we'll discuss in the next chapter, it really comes down to 'wants' and 'needs'. Neil and I classify Kayo as a 'want', so Neil pays for it from his gold card (more on that in the next chapter, too). However, we *are* Canberra Raiders supporters and, as their matches are rarely on the free 9Now streaming service or Channel 9 free-to-air TV, we could argue that it's a necessity for the duration of the NRL season.

Potential savings:

Per month	$115
Per year	$1380
Time saved on your mortgage	2 years and 4 months
Interest saved on your mortgage	$66,080

Subscription streaming services

I remember when Netflix first came on the scene. It was a game changer. Everyone was talking about it. Faster and more reliable internet has made streaming movies and TV shows both possible and popular, and we now take for granted the ability to watch whatever we want, whenever we want.

Unsurprisingly, demand for streaming services is growing, and many relied on them during those long lockdown weeks and months at the peak of the pandemic. According to the PwC

Australian Entertainment & media Outlook 2022–2026, over 75 per cent of households paid for a streaming service in 2021, with the average Australian household now spending $40 a month on 2.3 subscription services. Does that sound familiar?

The subscription trap

We all know how easy it is to sign up for the free trial and then end up paying for months because we forget to unsubscribe. It's only $10 a month, or $21, or whatever it is, so it doesn't seem like much in the scheme of things, but it adds up – and quickly.

According to Terry Flew, a professor of digital communication and culture at the University of Sydney, the amount we spend on entertainment is often hidden because we pay monthly and don't consider the annual cost.

'Many of these services are an automatic monthly deduction, which people don't take notice of as much as they would if they were to make a one-off physical payment,' he explained to *The Guardian*. 'It's the genius of the model.'

We are so used to subscription services that it's easy to forget we can still rent or buy movies, including online. If you only watch movies occasionally, this can work out much cheaper. It also means you have a greater choice in what you watch because you can purchase exactly what you want to watch rather than being limited by what's available on your chosen service. However, many streaming services offer exclusive series that you just can't get anywhere else. So, if you want to watch the fifth and final series of *The Marvellous Mrs. Maisel*, you'll probably need to sign up for a Prime Video subscription.

The problem, then, is that once you've taken out that subscription, it's hard to cancel. Last Christmas, our family festive experience was watching the movie *Die Hard*. My kids liked it so much that we watched all five films in the franchise. It worked out cheaper for us to subscribe to Disney Plus than to rent the original *Die Hard* movie as we had originally planned, but then life got busy. Four months and $60 later, we finally cancelled it. While admittedly we did watch the other four *Die Hard* movies, plus other shows during those four months (including the *Star Wars* spinoffs), it ended up costing us much more than we had intended to pay.

Most subscription services count on you doing what we did: forgetting to cancel. I've even forgotten I signed up for something in the first place – I only realised after I saw a name I didn't recognise on my credit card statement! It took me a while to work out what it was for, and longer again to then log in and cancel the subscription.

Here are a few tips and tricks for reducing money on subscriptions:

- **Don't sign up in the first place.** Decide to rent or buy only what you need (or engage in some free or frugal pursuits instead), and never enter into subscription services. If you never sign up, you'll never get caught paying for services you don't really need.

- **Diarise when to cancel – and set a reminder.** When you sign up for a free trial, go to your diary and immediately enter the date you want to cancel it. I use Google Calendar on my phone and usually schedule an alert for a day or two before.

- **Cancel early.** Whenever you cancel a subscription, it will usually continue until the next billing period. So in other words, as soon as you go, 'Oh, I really should get around to cancelling that subscription,' cancel it. Then make a point of enjoying the last week or two or three of your subscription.

- **Only have one subscription going at a time.** If you tend to watch the big headline series or shows, subscribe to one subscription service only. My mother-in-law did this with Paramount+. She signed up, watched all her favourite

NCIS episodes and then cancelled her membership. (Yes, she likes *NCIS* a lot.)

· **Share a subscription.** Save money by sharing a subscription with family members or others. However, be careful you don't get stuck paying for a subscription you no longer use but won't cancel because you're worried about offending the other person. Remember, too, that sharing a subscription is different to sharing a password. There is change afoot about the mechanics and legalities of sharing subscriptions with people in different residences, so check the fine print. If the intention is to have more than one person using an account, you will likely have to pay for that.

It's not wrong to spend money on Foxtel, Netflix or Spotify. I just want to challenge the idea that these subscriptions are essential. The reality is that satellite TV and streaming services are discretionary spending and, if you're paying the average of $40 a week, the cost adds up. Let's look at what you could save if you decided to cancel your subscriptions today and instead put that money straight onto your mortgage.

Potential savings:

Per month	$40
Per year	$480
Time saved on your mortgage	8 months
Interest saved on your mortgage	$24,627

It's not just TV

TV and cinema were the only forms of screen entertainment available in Australia for decades. These days there are many ways to access entertainment, even on mobile devices, with streaming and subscription services – and it's not just Netflix, Disney Plus and YouTube.

Want a break from ads? Many of the eight million Australians who use Spotify do, and they pay $11.99 a month individually or $18.99 as a family for the privilege. Could you handle listening to some short ads if it meant paying off your mortgage sooner? What is more important: listening to music uninterrupted or your financial freedom? Similarly, do you pay $14.99 a month to watch or listen to YouTube Premium, or are you okay with listening to some ads? If you like retro music and you're frugal, you can even get by with listening to CDs. Op shops, libraries and garage sales are filled with CDs, and I have found some great bargains over the years – and they used to be so expensive. Just stand in front of the CD shelf in an op shop and, assuming each CD originally cost $25, work out how much people must have spent on their CD collections.

Audiobooks are great for listening to in the car, particularly on long road trips, when commuting on public transport and working out. I love listening and learning while cooking dinner. Audible plans start at $16.45 a month, Scribd is $11.99 USD a month and Blinkist, which offers summaries of books and other sources, is $19.99 a month. Instead, you could listen to many podcasts – here's a plug for *The Joyful Frugalista* – for free. Your local library will also have a range of audiobooks available for loan digitally or on CD.

Having been gifted a Kindle, I enjoy using a Kindle Unlimited subscription at $13.99 a month as a sometimes treat. Another online digital resource is Kobo, also $13.99 a month. That said, I also enjoy reading books and ebooks for free from my local library, which I can search for and reserve online if choosing hardcopy or borrow and read digitally on my phone. Some local libraries have their own apps, but you can also use the Libby app for this.

Subscriptions are now required to be able to access many news sources. If you enjoy reading your local news or need to be informed about breaking news and commentary, then it can be hard *not* to subscribe. The problem is that subscriptions can be hard to cancel. News platforms often lure you with cheap short-term subscriptions, and when you go to cancel they offer you more short-term deals to keep you signed up. I had to make three phone calls to a particular news outlet before I was able to say no to the super special deals being offered for the very final time. As they do with ebooks and audiobooks, libraries offer free online and in-person access to a large range of newspapers and magazines. It can take some time to find the information, and it might not be in the format you are used to, but it is there – you might just need to ask a librarian for help. Finally, if you need access to a news source for work, consider asking your workplace to pay for it.

What else could you be doing with your free time?

Amy Dacyczyn, author of *The Tightwad Gazette*, categorised satellite TV as an unnecessary expense and a distraction from more important things in life. She suggested families could find plenty of entertainment and educational opportunities by instead reading books, playing games, spending time outdoors and participating in community or money-making activities. I first read *The Tightwad Gazette* over 15 years ago, and it profoundly influenced my decision to adopt a frugal lifestyle. It motivated me to re-examine my life, think about what I could do to earn more money and use my time more productively and intentionally. Dacyczyn's insight about satellite TV being inessential has saved me tens of thousands of dollars over the years. It led to me prioritising frugal activities like cooking things from scratch and fixing things rather than watching TV. It also inspired me to use my spare time to start blogging, which eventually led to bigger projects such as this book.

Did you know that couples with a TV in their bedroom have less sex? Now that I have your attention, instead of spending money (and time) on satellite and streaming services, what could you do that would bring you more sustainable joy and help pay your mortgage off? Here are some ideas:

- **Watch a DVD.** Yes, they still exist, and you can often buy them cheaply at op shops or garage sales. You can also borrow DVDs from your library (I did this often when my kids were little) or get them for free through your local Buy Nothing Project group.
- **Renovate your house.** Spend your evenings planning or doing your own renovations rather than watching others do it on TV.
- **Start a blog or channel.** Yes, some people still blog, although increasingly people are Instagramming or TikToking. Whatever your interest or passion, lean in and use this extra time to learn new skills.
- **Learn to play an instrument.** Have you ever considered learning to play the guitar, piano or another instrument? Ditch Netflix and learn to play. You don't have to pay for lessons if you don't want to, either – YouTube is full of free tutorials for all skill levels.
- **Study online.** Enrol in a course on something you've always wanted to learn about. Upskilling will help you in your career and broaden your horizons. Look for MOOCs (Massive Open Online Courses) that interest you. They're usually free, and you can learn anything from coding to cake decorating.
- **Learn a language.** Free resources such as Duolingo use gamification principles to make it easy and fun to learn a new language.

Of course, there are many other free activities you could be doing that include your partner, like cooking together in the kitchen, or playing board games, or maybe going for a walk in the bush or a bike ride. Maybe you could even (shock horror) talk to one another.

Sometimes you might want to indulge in TV. There are many free-to-air channels, as well as ABC iview, SBS On Demand, 9Now, 7plus, 10 play and other free streaming services to choose from. Many libraries also offer free access to streaming services, such as Kanopy and Beamafilm. I confess that I get addicted to TV easily – especially drama series – so I have to be careful. If I start watching something, I will have trouble turning it off. Knowing this about myself, I'm conscious of not just sitting down after dinner to start watching something because I know I am not likely to move off the sofa for several hours. My exception to this is watching movies with my sons as a family activity. They delight in selecting movies they know I probably won't like, and Neil and I delight in selecting 'cringe' movies for them. It's a lot of fun.

A frugal approach to fitness

Finder reports that 6.2 million Australians – that's 24 per cent of the population – have a gym membership, but half of those attend the gym less than once a week, and all up we waste $2.4 billion annually on unused gym memberships.

On average, Australians spend around $780 a year on gyms. Then there are the boutique gyms and their large prices; the Cremorne Club, which went to administration in April 2023, charged members $430 a month ($5160 a year). Many F45 franchises also experienced problems in 2023; they charged around $66 a month ($792 a year). Having a gym membership is not wrong, but it's important to be honest with yourself about how often you use it. If you don't have time in your busy schedule to go to the gym, spending a lot of money on an annual membership doesn't make sense.

It's possible to stay fit and healthy while also being fiscally responsible. Here are some of my tips for reducing your spend on subscription-based fitness:

- **Walk, walk and walk.** Before you sign up for something complex, consider this simple exercise. It can be very effective when done regularly. Best of all, as I mentioned in chapter 9, you may even save money on transport.

- **Take the stairs.** Where possible, take the stairs rather than the lift. My family always does this and we're always surprised by how much exercise we get as a result. I'm also surprised by how many people in our apartment complex take the lift for only one or two flights of stairs. Rather than driving to the gym and getting on a stepping machine, use what you have.

- **Pay per visit.** If you only intend to visit the gym or pool infrequently or semi-regularly, consider paying only for the sessions you actually attend. Some facilities have 10-session passes, while others offer casual rates that might be more cost-effective for you in the longer run.

- **Try parkrun.** One reason people like gyms is the community – parkrun is a free community 5 km event where you can walk, run, volunteer or even spectate. Over 470 parkruns take place every Saturday morning around Australia. Jump on parkrun.com.au to find one near you.

- **Exercise at home.** Simple bodyweight exercises such as push-ups, squats or lunges at home are free and effective. You can get creative and use water bottles or tinned food as weights when it's time to level up, or try incorporating resistance bands into your routine.

- **Find a workout channel you like.** I still remember when free-to-air TV broadcast aerobics in the morning. While some episodes make a lycra retro comeback from time to time, the good news is that you can find many workout channels online for free. YouTube is a great place to start, and no matter your preferred type of exercise – yoga, aerobics, circuit training or something else entirely – there's a channel to suit.

- **Play a sport.** While registration costs will be involved in playing a sport, they're often less than joining a gym, and being part of a team is a great way to stay accountable. You'll likely also make friends while doing something you enjoy.

Don't forget that there are often cancellation fees if you decide to end your gym membership early (even if you need to for health reasons), so make sure you check the fine print. As with streaming subscriptions, the money often comes directly out of your bank account or goes straight onto your credit card, and it can take some effort to decide to cancel the service.

Potential savings:

Per month	$65
Per year	$780
Time saved on your mortgage	1 year and 4 months
Interest saved on your mortgage	$39,130

Summary

- Streaming services are typically cheaper than satellite TV, even for sports watchers, and demand for them is growing.
- It's easy to sign up for a free trial and get trapped paying for a subscription, so make sure you set a reminder to unsubscribe – or just don't subscribe at all.

- There are lots of free and cheap ways to watch movies and TV series. Try your local library or Buy Nothing Project group for DVDs.
- There are many more productive things we could be doing than watching TV – and many of them are free.
- Around 24 per cent of Australians have a gym membership, but only half attend the gym more than once a week. However, there are many frugal ways to keep fit.

In this chapter I showed you how quickly subscription costs can add up and covered some great ways to stay entertained for less. Next I'm going to venture into the latte debates and help you to see how small changes to your habits can make a difference over time – and you don't have to give up coffee.

Chapter 11

The million-dollar coffee habit

I went to a housewarming a week after my first book, *The Joyful Frugalista*, was published.

'I saw you on television,' someone said.

'Oh, really?' I answered. 'Which channel?'

'I saw you on *The Project*,' he said.

I thought at first that he had made a mistake or that I had heard wrong because, though I'd had a bit of media (including a session on *Sunrise*), I hadn't been invited onto *The Project*. But it turned out that a clip in which I compared coffee and tea in a supermarket had, in fact, been on the program. As part of it, I'd said that you could save 'hundreds and thousands of dollars'.

'She must drink a lot of coffee,' the host of the show quipped. Everyone laughed.

I was mortified. I'd been ridiculed on national TV. However, although 'hundreds and thousands of dollars' of savings sounds like an outlandish claim, I knew I was right. I've crunched the numbers about coffee drinking, and the results might surprise you – they certainly surprised me.

In this chapter I'll show you how much a coffee habit can cost and explore the difference you can make to your mortgage by changing your habits.

Coffee sums

I have a confession to make: I don't drink coffee. I haven't had a full-strength coffee since 2009. I gave it up when I was pregnant with my first son and never resumed after he was born. I have never been a big coffee drinker, partly because I'm quite sensitive to caffeine, but also partly because of my frugal outlook on life. It didn't make sense to me to start each day paying for barista-made coffee.

Coffee is addictive. We know that. In our busy lives, with lack of sleep, work deadlines, children, fur babies and all sorts of things that exhaust us, for many of us it's coffee that keeps us going. Many of us struggle to function without it. I remember one year working during the Christmas–New Year period when the cafe at my work building had shut down and bumping into colleagues who looked like zombies. 'Where can I get good coffee?' was a common refrain.

But how much does your morning barista coffee cost you? It varies depending on the cafe, of course, and the type and size of coffee. Non-dairy milk, flavoured syrups and larger sizes will increase the price. Because it's addictive, it's hard to go without a morning cup of coffee. It also means that many people don't stop at one cup – they often drink two, three or maybe more. Then it's also easy to splurge on the temptations that go with it: egg and bacon rolls, muffins, choc-chip cookies and croissants. Assuming you buy *only one* cup of barista coffee each day at just $5, and none of those delicious treats, you will spend $35 week, or $1825 a year, on coffee.

What would the impact be if you didn't have that barista-made coffee every day and instead put the money onto your mortgage? I've done the sums, and I'm shocked at the true cost of a daily cup of coffee. If, rather than spending $5 a day on a coffee, you put an additional $152 a month onto your mortgage (that's $5 a day, multiplied by 365 days, then divided by 12), you could pay off your mortgage in 26 years and 11 months and save $84,456. In other words, you could own your home three years and one month sooner if you don't buy a coffee every day and instead put the cost onto your mortgage.

Potential savings:

Per week	$35
Per year	$1825
Time saved on your mortgage	3 years and 1 month
Interest saved on your mortgage	$84,456

The million-dollar coffee habit and your superannuation

Cutting out (or at least cutting down on) barista coffee can make a huge difference to the balance of your mortgage and save you stacks of money in interest over the life of your loan. However, if you invested in making additional contributions to superannuation the savings would be even greater, helped along by the magic of compound interest.

I calculate that if, over a working life of 42 years (and making assumptions about future performance based on past average performance), someone put $4 that would otherwise be spent on buying coffee with their mates every morning into their superannuation fund instead, they would retire with an extra $1.2 million in their account. Even though I understand the power of compound interest and was expecting the total to be high, I was surprised by the results of my calculations.

US finance author and commentator Suze Orman has come to a similar conclusion. In a viral video, she states that a daily coffee habit costs people $1 million over their lifetime. She calculated that the average American could amass $1 million in their Roth IRA account (the US equivalent of superannuation) if they gave up coffee and instead put more into that account. Suze notes that many people don't have a coffee just a few times a month – they have one every day, amounting to $100 USD monthly. Meanwhile, if someone chose to invest the same amount of money into a Roth IRA, over 40 years it would amount to $1 million USD.

'You need to think of it as: you are peeing $1 million down the drain as you are drinking that coffee,' she says on the video. 'Do you really want to do that? No!'

Suze then goes on to advise people to make their own coffee.

'Make it at home. Every penny counts,' she says.

Curbing the coffee spend

My good friend and frugal mentor Trish is a coffee lover. We talked about this chapter, surrounded by coffee vans, while she sold her bespoke denim handbags at a local market.

'I've already had two cups of coffee today,' she said. 'I brought them with me in my thermos.'

We both laughed. While I don't drink it anymore, I know that Trish makes great coffee. She invested in an espresso machine over a decade ago and even undertook a short barista course offered by the manufacturer. She loves her coffee and, in the long run, has found a frugal way to make her own – and make it well.

If you love coffee, consider doing something similar. It might, for example, be worth it to spend a little more right now and save a lot in the long run. Espresso machines have decreased considerably in price in recent years, and capsule coffee machines (around just

$80 at ALDI) have made coffee even cheaper, with Nespresso pods starting at 77 cents each and ALDI pods at just 44 cents each. Coffee plungers (also known as French presses) are common items in op shops, and they make a lovely, cheap drop when paired with your choice of beans. Or you can go retro and buy a stovetop espresso pot, which are super stylish, look great on the stovetop and have been used by generations of Italians to make high-quality coffee at home. You could always move to the much-maligned instant coffee, too, particularly if coffee is, to you, less about taste and more about function. Table 6 contains some estimations for cost per cup across the first year some of these options.

Table 6: Cost of a cup of black coffee

Method	Initial outlay	Cost per cup	Cost over a year (1 cup per day)
Cafe	$0	$5	$1,825
Espresso machine	$500	23 cents*	$583.95
Capsule coffee machine	$80	44 cents	$240.60
Stovetop espresso pot	$70	23 cents*	$153.95
French press	$30 (less at an op shop)	23 cents*	$113.95
Instant coffee	$0	7 cents**	$25.55

*assuming supermarket brand, pre-ground beans, 7g per cup
**assuming Moccona brand, 1.7g per cup

If it's the ritual and comfort of a hot drink that's important to you, you could even consider making the switch to tea. In 2018, I was invited to talk about saving money for a TV segment, and the producers asked me to calculate how much money I spent weekly on coffee. As I don't drink coffee, I did my calculations based on tea and was surprised to find that drinking tea is a much cheaper option. For comparison's sake, in table 7 I've shared some cost-per-cup calculations for a range of different kinds of tea.

Table 7: Cost of a cup of tea

Brand	Cost per cup
Cafe	$5
T2 English Breakfast ($12/25 bags)	72 cents
Twinings English Breakfast ($11/100 bags)	11 cents
Lipton Quality Black Tea ($5/100 bags)	5 cents
Dilmah Ceylon Tea ($5.10/100 bags)	5 cents
Bushell's Blue Label Tea Bags ($3.50 /100 bags)	4 cents
Coles Cup Tea Bags ($1.90/100 bags)	2 cents
ALDI Diplomat Tea Cup Bags ($1.79/100 bags)	2 cents
Lan-choo Loose Leaf Tea ($3.60/250g)	2 cents
Twinings Mango & Strawberry Infusions Tea ($3.00/10)	30 cents

A whole bag of tea is too strong for me, so Neil and I often share a single bag between two cups. Accordingly, our cups of ALDI tea, brewed at home, cost just 1 cent each. We're increasingly brewing loose tea in a pot rather than using a tea bag. I find that not only is this tea better quality and more enjoyable, but it is also more sustainable because it reduces packaging wastage from tea bags and leftover leaves can go straight into the worm farm.

If you feel you need a little help curbing the coffee habit, it can be helpful to use the same strategy I mentioned in chapter 4 when

I considered buying an ALDI doona cover set. I was so focused on paying off my mortgage by the end of that year that I would check my balance online every day. Still, some days I felt like I needed a chai latte, maybe with a snack, to get me through the afternoon. Often, as I was standing in line ready to put in my order, I realised that I didn't really need it. I would then go back to my desk and immediately transfer the cost of what I would have spent onto my mortgage.

Yes, you can do that. You can pay more on your mortgage anytime, even small amounts, and funnelling potential money leaks (even little ones, like the occasional coffee – or, as in my case, chai latte) straight onto the mortgage like this is a great way to get ahead. Some people even make it a habit to round up their purchases and put the money on their mortgage. For instance, if they buy a coffee for $4.80, they put the 20 cents that it would take to round that purchase up to $5 straight onto their mortgage.

Before you say, 'No way – I would *never* give up my coffee!' just stop and consider your priorities. Is enjoying a cup (or more) of barista-made coffee every day, rather than just occasionally, more important to you than owning your own home outright? Could you, would you, drink instant coffee (or use a French press, or just have a cup of supermarket-brand tea) some of the time, instead of having second cup of the good stuff, if it means owning your home sooner? What if it means being able to retire sooner, or with more money in your super fund?

Supporting small business

Small businesses need our support. In Australia, 95 per cent of our coffee shops are independent; in recent years, they've been doing it tough. Increases in energy costs, rent, coffee beans and dairy prices have seriously affected their bottom lines. So, if you value your local businesses, do continue to support them. What's important is to prioritise yourself and your financial wellbeing. Rather than avoiding coffee shops and cafes altogether, it's about having balance and ensuring you manage your discretionary spending well.

I once met with someone at a cafe who prided themselves on being frugal and refused to order anything (or let me pay for a coffee). That's their prerogative, but I do feel it is important to support small businesses, especially if you're taking up a table. With this in mind, I treat myself to a chai latte or cup of tea when having a coffee date with someone, and I often treat them as well. It's a great way to connect. A former colleague of mine aimed to have a coffee chat with someone new once a week as a form of networking; making those connections was important to them, so they invested both time and money in that, while also supporting small business.

'Wants' versus 'needs'

If we go back to Suze Orman's video, her central argument seems to hinge on 'wants' and 'needs'. As she says, if you spent your money only on 'needs' rather than on 'wants', 'you would find the money to invest in your retirement accounts' or 'get yourself out of credit card debt'.

The point is not that coffee is evil or that cafes are bad, but rather that buying a coffee is a form of discretionary spending. It's not something essential like putting food on the table, paying your bills or putting petrol in your car (assuming public transport can't meet your needs). Accordingly, when you're looking to cut costs and save money, barista-made coffee is often one of the easiest things to stop spending money on (caffeine addiction notwithstanding).

Financial planner Michael Miller and I have very different values when it comes to coffee. For me it's a discretionary item, a 'want', but for him it's a 'need.' Michael loves his coffee and has several local cafe owners as clients. For Michael, getting his morning coffee is a ritual. The aroma of roasted coffee, the time out from the office and the chat with his friendly barista make the experience special. Though there's no way Michael would go without his coffee, he agrees with me about the importance of good financial micro habits and believes it's the little things that add up. The difference is that Michael would prioritise curbing expenses in other ways, such as reducing subscriptions (as we discussed in chapter 10), over curtailing his coffee ritual.

We all have 'wants' that can get out of control. Maybe it's coffee, but it could be wine, chocolate bars, clothing, shoes, playing the pokies, dating apps or subscriptions. The trick is to notice when a 'want' is costing you more money than you would like it to – and to do something about it.

For example, I'm currently working to treat a bit of a bling addiction. An op shop near me sells fabulous earrings for $3 a pair (it used to be only $2). I found myself going there if I was feeling lost or down or having a bad day at work. It's not costing me much money, and I'm doing it all on my 'gold card' (more on that in a moment), but I've noticed that little bit of this retail therapy is becoming a crutch – and it isn't aligned with my frugal and sustainable values (or my minimalist aspirations). So, I'm having a bit of a jewellery pause to appreciate what I have before buying more.

A note on bottled water

I've been focusing on coffee and other 'wants' (as opposed to 'needs') in this chapter, but I'm continually shocked and amazed by the number of Australians who regularly buy bottled water. We have some of the cleanest and purest water in the world. It is such a blessing to have reliable tap water when so many people in the world live without safe water.

It costs around 1 cent per litre to get quality water out of a tap. Yet, according to a UN report, in 2021 Australians spent on average around $580 buying 504 litres of bottled water. Not only are Australians the second-highest consumers of bottled water per capita (behind Singapore), we also pay more for it than anyone else – despite tap water being available for free in many places.

The waste caused by plastic water bottles is staggering; according to Sustainability Victoria, Australians buy almost 15 billion plastic bottles a year, 53 per cent of which end up in landfill and 12 per cent back in the environment as litter.

If you want to save money to pay your mortgage off, you should not only focus on reducing your spending on 'wants', like coffee, but also on saying no to buying bottled water.

The gold card strategy for discretionary spending

One way to limit spending on 'wants' is to have a set allowance each fortnight. You can call it what you like: 'sanity allowance', 'beer money' or, as in my case, the 'gold card'.

Neil and I put $100 each a fortnight straight onto our Qantas Travel Money Cards. We got these cards, which are essentially reloadable prepaid debit cards, through our club memberships, and we collect Qantas Points when we use them. We particularly like that they *look* like credit cards (Neil's is gold, which is why we call them 'gold cards'), but they're not. When the money runs out, it's gone. The deal is that the money on each card can be spent on whatever Neil and I like, and we don't have to tell one another or justify our spending. So, if I want to buy bling at an op shop, even though I know I already have too much, I can. If Neil wants to shout his mates a round of beers, he can. We use it for personal spending, such as coffees or lunches with friends, online purchases or those times when we feel like buying lunch at work. Most importantly, it's all in the budget.

I asked Neil what he likes best about the gold card, and these were his words: 'I like the freedom to spend it on whatever I want: beers with the boys, a present for my wife, treats for the kids, indiscretions like coffees and the occasional takeaway, ice-cream – whatever.'

Personally, I love, love, *love* the freedom of having a small pot of money that is just mine. As a domestic violence survivor, I believe in the importance of always having a private 'fuck-off fund'. The fact that I have one and don't have to hide it or share details of what I spend it on proves that I'm now in a loving and supportive relationship. I like being able to buy birthday presents for Neil without him knowing the details. And he, in return, is often a bit naughty and uses his card to take me out to dinner – because that's what he wants to do.

I also feel that the gold card has helped us have a better relationship. Arguments about money are so often over small things, especially when finances are tight. Having your own defined budget for discretionary spending – and a sense that you have freedom with and ownership over your money – helps build trust and avoid arguments over petty things.

We aren't the only ones to use the gold card strategy. Property investor and innovation superstar Irene Zhen and her partner each give themselves $150 a fortnight. (Maybe Neil and I should raise our rate...) They put their money onto an ING Orange Everyday card and use their bright orange card as their gold card. As this goes to show, you can use whatever card you want as a gold card – just make sure there are no account, transaction or withdrawal fees. It doesn't even have to be gold (or orange). The most important thing is that you have a clear and defined way of assigning a budget for discretionary spending.

Summary

- If you spend $5 on just one cup of coffee a day, that adds up to $1825 a year. Of course, you would spend even more if you have an extra cup or two throughout the day or succumb to the temptation of cafe food.

- If you put that money onto your mortgage instead of having a barista-made coffee every day, you could pay your home off three years and one month faster, saving $84,456 in interest.

- A cup of Moccona instant coffee costs 7 cents and a cup of tea made with an ALDI teabag costs 2 cents, compared with $5 (or more) for a cup of barista-made coffee.

- Coffee is a want rather than a need (although it might feel like a need first thing on a Monday morning).

- Curbing habitual discretionary spending (coffee, alcohol, bottled water, earrings and so on) will help you to turbocharge your mortgage repayments.

Cafe owners need our support. So, if you value making connections and networking over coffee, don't cut it out completely; just make sure that you prioritise your financial wellbeing.

You don't have to cut coffee out completely to make big savings, but you may need to think about how and when you indulge if your mortgage is your priority. I'm going to show you how to make more savings in the next chapter – this time with some cheap and clever cleaning hacks.

Chapter 12

Frugalista cleaning hacks

Do you remember that ad about the new mum who had people come to visit her but was stressed out about the state of her loo? Many of us want our homes to be clean and worry about what others think of us. Having a neat, clean home can be satisfying. The problem is that we spend billions of dollars on cleaning products, many of which are toxic and bad for the environment – and some are really just hope in a bottle. Pre-COVID, Australians spent around $4 billion a year on cleaning – and it's a growing trend, with around a third of us buying more cleaning products since the start of the pandemic as a result of spending more time at home during lockdown. The good news is that I've found many alternatives that can save you money and help the environment.

I believe that, on average, these hacks can save a family up to $50 a month. It's difficult to quantify this as people spend differently. Some people prefer things like fancy dishwasher tablets, while others will just wash their dishes with dishwashing liquid. However, I know that my ability to make my own cleaning items is one of the secret weapons that enables me to stick to a $100 weekly food and grocery budget. I also feel secure that my home is not filled with harmful chemicals.

Potential savings:

Per month	$50
Per year	$600
Time saved on your mortgage	1 year and 1 month
Interest saved on your mortgage	$30,517

In this chapter, I'll share with you some of my top hacks and recipes for ways to clean your home and save. How many you adopt will affect how much you can save in this area of your weekly spending – and how much you can allocate to extra mortgage repayments.

Bicarbonate of soda

Let me tell you about the power of bicarbonate of soda. A 500 g packet of bicarb at Woolworths costs $2.45. And it costs even less if you buy it in bulk: if you're super keen on cleaning, you could invest in a 6.1 kg bag from Costco for $10.99. 'Hang on, how much will I need?' you might ask. Well, I find it useful in so many ways that I expect you'll be going back for more.

No matter how many times you run cups and mugs through a dishwasher, you'll invariably find that coffee and tea stains keep deepening. You can remove these stains by making a paste combining a tablespoon of bicarb with a small amount of water. Apply the paste and watch the stains vanish. If you don't have bicarb with you, perhaps if you're at work, you can use salt; I find it's not as effective as the bicarb method, but it still works fine.

Bicarb is alkaline and white vinegar is acidic. Both are powerful cleaning agents on their own, but when combined they create a chemical reaction that's useful for cleaning hard-to-move stains. You can use this to your advantage on difficult-to-shift surface marks, such as hard water stains in the shower, by sprinkling bicarb and vinegar onto the surface until the combination fizzes. Then, use a stiff brush to scrub off the stains.

Here are a few more methods of using bicarb to clean both cheaply and effectively.

Dishwasher tablets

With the cost of dishwasher tablets rising, it makes sense to make them yourself. And it's not just about the cost to your wallet – many dishwasher tablets also aren't good for the environment. Many tablets are covered with the synthetic polymer polyvinyl alcohol (PVA), which reduces the amount of water needed; however, not all PVA breaks down totally, with some of it becoming microplastics.

The good news is that you can make your own dishwasher tablets simply and easily using ingredients you can find in the supermarket aisle.

Dishwasher tablets

Ingredients:

- 1 cup bicarbonate of soda
- 1 cup Lectric Washing Soda
- 1/4 cup Epsom salts (or cooking salt)
- 1/4 cup citric acid
- 1/2 tablespoon dishwashing liquid
- orange vinegar (recipe in the next section) or white vinegar to mix

Method:

1. Combine all dry ingredients in a bowl.
2. Add in the dishwashing liquid and then gradually stir in the vinegar, around half a teaspoon at a time. The mixture will fizz as you add in the vinegar. This is normal.
3. Once the mixture is crumbly and wet, spoon into a plastic or silicon icetray.
4. Press down firmly and allow to harden overnight.

Store in a dry, airtight container and use one per wash as you would with commercial dishwasher tablets.

Stubborn surface stain cleaner

Many people swear by white alkaline pastes that are used for cleaning mouldy or water-stained surfaces in bathtubs, showers and kitchens. You can make something similar at home using a few simple ingredients.

Homemade Gumption

Ingredients:

- 1/2 cup bicarbonate of soda
- 2–3 tablespoons of liquid Castile soap or dishwashing liquid
- 1 teaspoon essential clove oil
- water

Method:

1. Mix the bicarb, dishwashing liquid and clove oil together in a bowl until it forms a paste.
2. Add water slowly, constantly stirring, until you get a Gumption-like paste. The mixture should be thick and creamy but still spreadable.

To use the paste, apply it to the surface you want to clean and scrub with a sponge or cloth. The bicarb will help to remove dirt and stains, while the clove oil will provide a natural fragrance while disinfecting. (You could use tea-tree oil instead or omit it altogether if you prefer.) You could even spray on some orange vinegar (more on that next) for an even stronger cleaning solution. Rinse the surface thoroughly with water after cleaning.

If you have trouble with soap scum and water marks (or you're just sick of how quickly it builds up), you can cheat by investing in a small plastic squeegee. It should cost you just a couple of dollars, and if you hang it in your shower and use it to wipe down surfaces after every use, your shower screens will stay free of build-up for much longer.

Drain unblocker

The best method of unblocking drains is to avoid blocking them in the first place, so refrain from pouring oils and fats down the sink, and scrape leftovers off plates before washing them. However, if you do have a blocked drain, before you call the plumber or resort to highly toxic drain cleaners – some of which may even harm your plumbing infrastructure – try this simple trick using bicarb, vinegar and boiling waters.

Start by pouring a couple of cups of boiling water down the affected drain, and then sprinkle about half a cup of bicarb down the drain. After you've let that sit for a few minutes, pour a cup of vinegar down too. Allow that chemical reaction to take place undisturbed for up to 15 minutes, and then pour several more cups of boiling water down the drain to wash away anything that has been dislodged.

Orange peels

Orange oil is a common ingredient in cleaners, especially in eco-friendly cleaners that are tough on dirt and grime. The oil from oranges has natural antibacterial and antifungal properties, which means it's perfect for cleaning in the home – and it smells nice, too.

Here are some ways to use the power of oranges with cleaning products that are both easy and cheap to make. Never waste orange peels or spend $5 on a spray cleaning product again.

Spray products

The first recipe I have to share is for a basic orange vinegar, which you can use as a general kitchen and bathroom spray.

Orange vinegar

Ingredients:

- 2 clean glass jars (I like to use leftover pasta sauce jars)
- leftover orange peels (pith and fruit removed)
- white vinegar
- clean spray bottle (you can use old window cleaner bottles and the like for this)

Method:

1. Fill a jar (preferably one that has just come out of the dishwasher as it will be clean and sterile) with orange peels.
2. Pour enough white vinegar into the jar to cover the peels. It's important to ensure that all of the orange peels are fully covered.
3. Put the lid on the jar tightly and place it in a dark place (for example, a cupboard) and allow it to sit for several weeks.
4. Place a Chux or cheesecloth into the mouth of a funnel over another clean glass jar.
5. Filter the contents of the jar by pouring it through the funnel into the second jar.

6. Pour this filtered concentrate into a leftover spray bottle to around two-thirds full.
7. Top the spray bottle up with water.

To use, simply spray on the dirty surface and wipe to remove. This spray is great for things like stovetops and benches that get sticky or greasy, and it also works well for glass, stainless steel, ceramics and tiles. However, it's important to avoid wood, marble, granite and lacquered surfaces.

You can make an even stronger spray by combining orange vinegar with Lectric Washing Soda (available in larger supermarkets). I call this powerful household cleaning agent my 'miracle spray' for a reason!

Miracle spray

Ingredients:

- 1 cup boiling water
- 3 tablespoons Lectric Washing Soda
- 2 cups room-temperature water
- 300mL undiluted orange vinegar
- 4 tablespoons dishwashing liquid

Method:

1. Combine the Lectric Washing Soda with boiling water in a large bowl or jug and stir to dissolve.
2. Add water, orange vinegar and dishwashing liquid, and stir to combine.
3. Pour into spray bottles.

This is perfect for cleaning things like greasy range hoods or other oily or dirty areas. Simply spray on and wipe off using a sponge or cloth.

Toilet cleaner

Many toilet cleaners are unnecessarily toxic, but a cheap and easy alternative is to refill old bottles with your own cleaner. Not only will this reduce the amount of plastic going to landfill, but it will also save you money.

For a basic, everyday cleaner, make a batch of miracle spray using six tablespoons of dishwashing liquid (rather than four as in the original recipe). Pour this into an old toilet-cleaner bottle and squirt into the rim as required.

If you've got some stains that are proving harder to shift, use the combined powers of oranges, vinegar and bicarb. Simply sprinkle a couple of tablespoons of bicarb around the bowl, spray with orange vinegar and scrub hard. Let it sit for a few minutes and flush.

Other household cleaners

Lots of other household products are very effective cleaners – and you've probably already got everything you need to use them. Next I'm going to take you through cleaning products you can make cheaply and easily at home using ingredients that you've probably already got in your pantry, bathroom or linen cupboard.

Spot cleaner

Did you know that toothpaste is a good spot cleaner? Yes, toothpaste. It has a good lather, it's non-toxic and it's super cheap. You'll never buy a bottle of cream cleaner again!

I regularly use budget white toothpaste in the bathroom for removing yellow stains under toilet seats and cleaning up the vanity. It's also great for removing marks from walls, including light bumps from moving house and uncommissioned artworks from kids.

To use, add half a fingernail of toothpaste onto a damp cloth (or toilet paper) and rub it over the surface. Rub on and wipe off – done!

Tile cleaner

My kitchen floor has white tiles that show the dirt easily. Consequently, I need to wash the floor often. Adding just a tablespoon of methylated spirits to half a bucket of hot water is the easiest and cheapest way to make a good tile cleaner that I have come across. It even dries quickly. This tip comes courtesy of my frugal friend Trish.

Leather conditioner and wooden furniture polish

Leather products can dry out or lose their shine. To keep them in good condition without spending loads of money, apply a small amount of coconut oil to the leather using a soft cloth.

Additionally, if you happen to own fabulous mid-century wooden furniture or other heirlooms, it's important to take care of them. The good news is that it doesn't have to be difficult or expensive. This basic polish using olive oil and lemon juice will keep in a clean jar for several months. To use it, simply dab a little onto a soft cloth and rub into hard wooden furniture.

Basic furniture polish

Ingredients:

- 1/4 cup olive oil
- 1/4 cup lemon juice

Method:

1. Pour the olive oil and lemon juice into a clean jar.
2. Shake until combined.

The following linseed oil polish is particularly good for darker-coloured wooden furniture. Linseed oil can help nourish and protect wood furniture, and it's also used as a decking oil. You can find linseed oil in hardware stores such as Bunnings.

Linseed oil furniture polish

Ingredients:

- 1/2 cup linseed oil
- 1/4 cup white vinegar
- 10–15 drops of lemon or cedarwood oil

Method:

1. Pour the linseed oil, white vinegar and essential oils into a clean jar.
2. Shake until combined.

Much like you would with the basic furniture polish, dab a little of this onto a soft cloth and apply directly to wooden furniture.

Jewellery cleaners

Never pay to have your jewellery professionally cleaned again – or spend money on sprays, polishes or wipes – with these cleaning hacks. Several of these suggestions make use of products I've already introduced, but know at least one will surprise you!

Before you get started, a quick note: be careful immersing jewellery set with sparkly stones (especially faux gemstones that may have been glued on) in hot water, as it might cause the stones to come out. I experienced this myself with a beautiful retro paste necklace.

Make gold and gold-plated jewellery sparkle again by placing it into a ceramic or glass bowl, sprinkling over some bicarb and salt, then covering it with boiling water. After it's had a chance to sit in the solution for a few minutes, and when the water isn't too hot to touch, remove and polish the jewellery with a soft cloth.

Silver and silver-plated jewellery takes a different treatment. Start by selecting a ceramic or glass bowl, then put a sheet of aluminium foil, shiny side up, in the bottom. Place your silver and silver-plated jewellery on top of the foil and sprinkle it with bicarb before covering the bowl's contents with boiling water. Then, watch in amazement as dull and tarnished silver brightens. Remove, dry and lightly polish with a silver cloth.

Pewter items are harder to clean than gold and silver. It takes persistence and a fair amount of hand polishing, but one of the most effective products to use is tomato sauce. Yes, tomato sauce that you put on sausage rolls and meat pies. Just cover the pewter items in tomato sauce and allow to sit overnight so the acid in the sauce has time to take effect. The next day, rinse the tomato sauce off with water and polish. Repeat as necessary.

Useful household materials

Did you know that harmful bacteria such as salmonella, E. coli and Listeria can thrive in dishwashing sponges because they're moist and porous? And do you really want to think about all the paper towels and disposable cleaning cloths you throw out every year?

The solution: cut up old clothing that is beyond repair and use that for cleaning instead. Depending on how you use this material, you can either wash and reuse them (for example, after dusting) or throw them out (after cleaning the toilet), reducing the risk of harmful bacteria growing and spreading while also reducing your contribution to landfill.

Here are some of my favourite fabrics for cleaning around the home:

- Commonly used for jackets in outdoor clothing because it's lightweight, durable and dries quickly, **synthetic fleece** (typically made from polyethylene terephthalate, PET) is one of the best cleaning fabrics you will find. Rather than simply throwing them out, cut up old jackets with stains, tears or broken zips and use them for cleaning. I cut up one of my sons' too-small, stained and broken old micro-fleece jacket to use on shower screens and it works a treat – particularly paired with the bicarb and vinegar combination discussed earlier in this chapter.

- Threadbare **flannel and flannelette** pyjamas and sheets with tears or stains are not always worth repairing. Cut them up to use for cleaning instead. The soft fabric is great for dusting, polishing furniture, stainless steel appliances and jewellery, as well as for general-purpose bench wiping.
- **T-shirt material** is also great for general-purpose cleaning. It can be particularly handy for cleaning paintbrushes if you're renovating too (see chapter 14 for more).
- The reverse, soft side of **tracksuit fleece** is great to use as a whiteboard eraser – better than any other product I have found. You can also use it for dusting.
- **Denim** is a hardwearing fabric and can be used for cleaning tough surfaces such as floors and benchtops. I also use a small piece of denim fabric for sharpening razor blades.

Materials for mirror cleaning

I'm slightly obsessive about clean mirrors. I feel that most people have cleaning tasks they prefer doing, and cleaning mirrors is mine. (It's definitely not vacuuming.) Depending on what you have on hand, here are a few different methods for cleaning mirrors.

You know how when you touch newspapers you end up with smudges on your hands? You'd think newspaper would leave marks on glass and mirrors, but surprisingly it's one of the best cleaning materials for mirrors because the oils in the papers naturally pick up dirt and grime. Simply scrunch up some dry newspaper and wipe it over your mirrors to remove most marks. If there are stubborn stains (for example, hardened flecks of toothpaste), slightly dampen the newspaper and scrub it off. You can then use fresh newspaper to dry and polish once the stains have been removed.

Face washers also work well for cleaning mirrors, especially in the bathroom. After someone has had a shower and the mirrors in the bathroom are foggy, use a face washer to wipe them down. The steam will help lift any sticky stains (especially those toothpaste flecks) and leave your mirror clean and streak-free.

My favourite way to clean mirrors is with a microfibre cloth. It easily removes fingerprints, dust and grime – plus, unlike using a commercial spray-on product, microfibre doesn't leave streaks. If there are stubborn marks that need a bit more care, you can remove them with a dampened microfibre cloth, and then use a dry cloth to remove any streaks. For super stubborn marks or stains, dampen the cloth with methylated spirits and rub until clear.

Summary

- Before spending a fortune on commercial cleaning products, try making and using your own sustainable products at home. You could save around $50 a month (conservatively), and you'll also help to save the environment from unnecessary landfill and toxic substances.

- Bicarb is one of the cheapest and most versatile cleaning products you can buy. It's even better when combined with white vinegar.

- Boost the power of white vinegar by infusing it with orange oil from leftover orange peels. The resulting orange vinegar can form the basis of several powerful cleaning products and even be used with bicarb or Lectric Washing Soda for extra impact.

- There are plenty of household products that can help you with your with cleaning. Toothpaste, for example, isn't just for cleaning your teeth; you can use it for cleaning many items in your bathroom and home, and even for tidying up light scrapes on walls.

• Before you throw out any old clothes or other fabric, consider if they could be cut up and used for cleaning. You may be surprised at how effective many textiles are.

As you can see from all of these handy tips and tricks, there are so many ways to clean your home without all those expensive (and sometimes toxic) products many of us rely on. Now that I've explored some ways of *saving* money, in the next chapter I'm going to show you some ways you might be able to *make* additional money for your mortgage.

Chapter 13

Make some extra money for your mortgage

Owning your own home is empowering. It's yours, and that gives you more agency to live your life on your terms. A good example of this is using your home to earn extra cash, which in turn will help you pay down your mortgage.

Some of the ideas I set out in this chapter are simply ways of making a little extra money with your space, while others are for side hustles: micro-businesses that you can carry out on the side of your main business. You might be surprised by all the ways you can earn additional income to pay off your mortgage!

Make your space make you money

Before we look at side hustles, let's think about how you might be able to use your home to make some additional money. Many of us have extra space *just sitting there*. What if you could monetise it and pay off that mortgage sooner?

Get a housemate

Many of us value our privacy, and when we move out of the family home, having our own space feels like luxury. However, sharing your space – even if only for a while – will help you get ahead on your mortgage and save big.

Having a housemate means that someone else is helping you pay your mortgage. Depending on the area you're in and the demand, you might find that their contribution covers quite a lot. Not only that, but they will also help contribute to shared expenses such as energy as well. Say you buy a two-bedroom apartment for $600,000 and rent out a second bedroom for $350 per week. That will give you an extra $1516 per month to pay on your mortgage – plus you get someone to help share the cost of utilities. You may even be able to claim a tax deduction.

With record-low vacancy rates for rentals in many cities, now is a great time to get a housemate. Do you have a spare room filled with junk? I used to have one like that in my previous house: a graveyard of memories and unused gym equipment. I sold some and then gave much of it away through my local Buy Nothing Project group, and then I rented out the room, earning thousands of dollars.

Maybe the thought of having someone strange in your home fills you with dread. Perhaps scenes from the classic *He Died with a Felafel In His Hand* play over in your mind. My advice here is to carefully check the references of potential housemates. These days, social media makes it easier to learn a bit about applicants, including whether you have friends and interests in common. Look at having a housemate as an opportunity meet new people. You may end up making lifelong friendships.

Technology makes it increasingly easy to find flatmates or house-mates. There are websites such as flatmates.com.au as well as local Facebook groups. You could also try putting up a poster at work or on an online classifieds page.

My friend Dan took advantage of a first home buyer grant and bought a two-bedroom unit in mid-2022. He lived by himself for the first six months and then, as he wasn't using it, decided to rent out the second bedroom. Dan says he was partly motivated by news of the housing crisis but also wanted a bit of company. He advertised on flatmates.com.au and a local Facebook group during February, when there was peak interest in housing where he lived. Dan had 80 people interested, and 48 walked through the door to view the apartment. The large volume of people allowed him the luxury of choosing who suited him the best. He didn't use the interest as an excuse to put up the rent, offering it at $290 a week (despite a real estate agent giving him an estimate of $350 a week).

'I was more interested in the person, and I get paid enough,' he said.

The rent from the housemate pays close to half of his mortgage repayments, which are $1450 a fortnight, and all bills aside from water are shared equally between Dan and his housemate. He claims 50 per cent of the apartment as an investment, which means he can get a tax deduction for things such as depreciation on fixtures and maintenance around the apartment. The arrangement works well, and lack of privacy isn't an issue.

'Once you become an adult, you generally learn to respect other people's boundaries,' he said. 'We get along well. If someone makes a mess, you clean it up. Once a week, someone gets the motivation and vacuums. We don't have a roster; I always thought they were over the top and didn't allow for the flexibility of life such as travel with work.'

Try Airbnb

If a long-term housemate isn't right for you, could you instead rent out a room in your home from time to time to earn extra cash? Neil and I did for several years, listing a room in our apartment on Airbnb as we paid the mortgage off.

I'll be honest and say I never thought I would do something like this. I thought it would be too much work, that my home wouldn't be good enough or that it would be hard to share a house with a stranger. However, a neighbour in my apartment complex did it. This neighbour moved to Canberra for work but frequently returned to Sydney to be with family, so his apartment was often vacant. After many discussions with him about how he managed it, Neil and I decided to give it a shot and rented out a spare room on the weekends when my children weren't with us, quickly reaching Superhost status. As our apartment was minutes from the light rail and within walking distance to the Australian National University, we hosted many fascinating academics and students. One time we hosted a graduate student from Princeton who was studying philosophy, and another time we hosted the father of a girl I went to primary school with.

We stopped hosting from our home during COVID as my husband has autoimmune vulnerabilities, but we continued to host for several more years in one of our investment properties. We earned around the same amount of money hosting for two nights as we would have for having a housemate in our apartment all week. Depending on where you are and how you market it, you could even earn more. A friend who splits her time between an inner-city apartment and a vineyard recently told me she can earn up to $350 a night with her Airbnb.

It's important to understand the legalities and restrictions of Airbnb hosting before you do it. In some areas, local planning approval is required to provide short-stay accommodation. Some apartment complexes also have rules regarding Airbnb hosting, and while it's not always clear if they are legally enforceable, it can certainly lead to conflict with neighbours and the body corporate. When hosting in my home, I view having an Airbnb guest as no different to having a friend come and visit. However, I also value my relationships with neighbours and ensure that I vet potential guests carefully. Thankfully, as Airbnb has an inbuilt peer-review mechanism, this is fairly easy.

According to Airbnb, Australian hosts can earn on average $11,500 a year. Note that you might need to pay tax on this amount, and it might be a good idea to get tax advice before you start. I assess these figures as on the high side and probably not for a spare back bedroom in a suburban area. But just for fun, let's take these figures and look at the savings you could make on your mortgage with this extra income.

Potential income:

Per month	$958.33
Per year	$11,500
Time saved on your mortgage	12 years
Interest saved on your mortgage	$313,486

Host a student

For nearly six years in the 2000s, my ex-husband and I hosted international students as part of homestay programs. We got to meet some amazing students from Colombia, Thailand, Japan, Korea and China, and we found it to be a great way to connect with students from around the world and learn about their cultures.

At the time, Australia was experiencing a sudden influx of international students, and on-campus accommodation options were limited. We were just a short bus ride away from the University of Canberra and the configuration of our house made us ideal homestay hosts – and while the money wasn't the only reason we welcomed guests into our home, it certainly helped.

Though they're less common today, homestay arrangements do still exist, and you can explore the possibilities through the Australian Homestay Network. Income from hosting students varies greatly depending on the arrangement with the institution, the cost of food and additional energy costs. In general, I believe you could earn between $150 and $200 per week hosting a student. Though the financial advantage is smaller than potential income from Airbnb or even a housemate, if you're within an easy commute to a university or higher education provider, a homestay arrangement might work for you.

Potential income:

Per month	$650
Per year	$7800
Time saved on your mortgage	9 years and 4 months
Interest saved on your mortgage	$251,513

Rent out a car space

When I was single parenting, my morning routine of dropping kids off at childcare and getting to work was crazy. I had limited time and mental bandwidth to worry about finding a car space near work every morning, so when I saw an ad on the work classifieds site to rent a space from someone who lived in a nearby apartment complex, I grabbed it.

With car parks becoming increasingly scarce – and expensive – demand for private parking spaces has shot up. If you're already making savings by going without a car (as discussed in chapter 9) or you have more parking space than you need, you could earn extra money by renting your space out.

Parkhound is a platform that connects private parking spaces with people who need somewhere to park. It's even recently been added to NSW's Park'nPay app, which allows users to search and pay for car spaces in real time. According to Parkhound, depending on a number of different factors, you can earn up to $5400 a year by renting out an extra car space. Using the 'easy money' calculator on the platform's website, I calculated that I could earn $208.75 a month – that's an extra $2505 a year – by renting out my car space using Parkhound.

Parkhound isn't the only platform that provides this service, with other marketplaces for storage and parking including Share with Oscar, KERB, Spacer and Carparkit. At present, most parking marketplaces operate in major capital cities and have limited availability in regional towns and cities, but check out what's on offer – you might be surprised.

Potential income:

Per month	$208.75
Per year	$2505
Time saved on your mortgage	4 years
Interest saved on your mortgage	$110,069

Get side hustling

There are many stories of people who have built empires from their computers while living with their mums and dads. Musicians have started bands in parents' garages. Some people have even become social media influencers from their share house bedrooms. In general, however, it's much easier to start and run your own home-based side hustle or business when you don't have to ask permission from the owner.

There are infinite ways that you can use your skills, hobbies and interests to net a little more money for your mortgage – and sometimes a side hustle can even become a main hustle. In the rest of this chapter I'm going to walk you through some side hustles that I've seen in action. Could any suit you?

With so many variables (such as demand and market saturation, skill, commitment and more), the return on these activities can vary greatly. I've indicated where possible what kind of compensation you might be able to expect, but it's important to think carefully and consider whether a side hustle is going to be worth it for you. For further information (and inspiration) on how to set up a business from scratch, check out my book *The Joyful Startup Guide*.

Grow fruit and vegetables

One of my favourite personal finance books was published in 1926 by George S. Clason. It's called *The Richest Man in Babylon*. Clason believed that owning your own home is a cornerstone to financial success – and happiness – and in a passage borrowing from scripture he discusses how eating the figs and grapes from one's own trees and vines brings gladness to one's heart. What Clason didn't write about, however, is that growing your own fruit and vegetables can not only bring you joy, it can help earn you money as well.

The most obvious way to monetise growing food is by eating it yourself. Cut down on your grocery bill by growing fruits, vegetables and berries that you like to eat and that you would normally spend money to buy. You don't have to have a big, sunny backyard to grow crops, although space and quality soil certainly help. I live in an apartment with shady balconies, but I still manage to grow parsley, rocket, spring onions and the virtually indestructible aloe vera. Any surplus from your garden can be made into pickles or jams – and they often make good gifts. You can also sell your excess produce. You can easily earn the equivalent of $20 a week from growing your own produce, even in a small space.

Mia Swainson, author of *Happy Planet Living*, President of the Canberra Environment Centre and a member of the ACT Climate Council, is a proud environmentalist with a rambling garden full of lots of edible goodies. Every year she makes beautiful jams using excess produce from her garden and gives them as gifts for Christmas and other events. I love her raspberry jam and treasure her homemade presents. Not only does Mia's gardening and preserving help the environment, but it also means she can spend less money on gifts.

Mia isn't the only person to benefit financially from her gardening. Her youngest son has an entrepreneurial spirit and took to harvesting and selling her crops to neighbours when he was eight years old. He did a roaring trade before she realised he'd sold what she was planning to cook later in the week. While she loves his entrepreneurial spirit, she thinks it's a bit unfair.

'I grew the vegetables,' she said to me, laughing. 'I'm the one who has done all the work!'

While Mia has pressed pause on her son's entrepreneurial ambitions (for now), I love that he doesn't feel the sort of social inhibition about door-to-door selling that many adults do. Personally, I would love to buy fresh vegetables from a neighbour! It saves using petrol on a trip to the shops, and it's just as good as picking from your own backyard. If you don't want to sell to your neighbours, you could consider selling at local markets. Alternatively, you could swap food with other gardeners or just reap the good karma from simply giving your excess produce to your neighbours.

Potential income:

Per week	$20
Per year	$1040
Time saved on your mortgage	1 year and 8 months
Interest saved on your mortgage	$51,309

Make your creative skills pay

If you have an artistic streak or some other creative pursuit, why not put that to use and earn some extra money? Online portals and social media platforms such as Etsy and Instagram make it easy to sell things online, and fetes and markets offer local artists and crafters opportunities to get their work – and business – out there.

When she's not travelling, my frugal friend Trish (the coffee-lover you met in chapter 11) loves to sew. When her daughter moved out, Trish wasted little time in converting the newly spare room into a new sewing room. She started making quilts and other lovely things from small pieces of fabric, which then morphed into a desire to create something beautiful and sustainable out of old jeans.

Denim is a hard-wearing fabric, but people tend to throw out jeans when they get thin in certain places, the zips break or they need other sorts of repairs. Trish got her hands on old jeans through her Buy Nothing Project group and began fashioning them – zips, buttons, pockets and all – into beautiful bespoke bags. She started selling to friends and taking individual orders, before taking a stall at a school fete. The success of that stall gave her the confidence to sell at more markets, and she's now a regular at local fetes, craft markets and sustainability gatherings.

Having watched Trish sew and sell her products through her business Upcycled by Trish, I can see the joy she gets from connecting her unique designs with people who appreciate them. She's an astute businesswoman and she has a natural flair for sales. However, her main motivation is creating beautiful bags from fabric that would otherwise go to landfill and then selling them to people who will use them. Her unique bags are treasured by the eco-conscious who love fashion.

It's not just creative products that can sell, either. You can also make some money from providing highly skilled services from your home if you have the skills and set-up. My friend Jen Seyderhelm is a radio host and podcaster who teaches podcasting and produces podcasts. She has converted a garage flat into a cool retro-style insulated room that's perfect for recording and podcasting. Jen says that professional podcast editors can charge around $70 an hour for their work, and in my experience they can sometimes charge more. There's also a growing market for podcast production (which goes beyond editing to include coming up with topics and securing talent) and video editing. Do you have a spare room and a skill set like this that you can make money from? This could be a way for you to use your home and your skills to make some extra cash for your mortgage.

Become a pet breeder

Australia has one of the highest pet ownership rates in the world, with more pets than humans. Around 69 per cent of Australian households own at least one pet. With high demand for pets, there is also demand for people to breed them. I'm often astounded by what people will pay for their pets. Being a prizewinning breeder can be lucrative. It's also something that you can do from your home.

Cathy Potter was made redundant from her construction job in 2021 due to COVID, but an unexpected and lifechanging opportunity came her way instead when she decided to go to Queensland to visit her daughter. Due to lockdowns she was unable to return home for three months, but while she was in Queensland she met a dog breeder. She came home with a breeding pool of seven dogs. Cathy now specialises in breeding poodle varieties including moodles (Maltese and poodle cross) and bichoodles (toy poodle and Bichon Frisé cross). She loves her puppies and raises them in a loving home. She belongs to Responsible Pet Breeders Australia and takes great care in placing her puppies with families that will care for them.

'It's not a quick buck,' warns Cathy. 'You have the stress of deliveries and things can go wrong – you must be prepared for that financially and emotionally. You don't become a breeder to make money; you become a breeder for the love of it.'

That said, now that Cathy's seven breeding females are producing pups, her business is profitable. Still, around a third of her income from puppy sales pays for costs such as food and grooming. Then there are additional costs for vet checks, advertising and washing bedding – not to mention the many sleepless nights she endures while caring for her dogs.

Engage in the second-hand economy

Ever bought something from Gumtree or Facebook Marketplace? The appetite for second-hand items is huge – and I predict it'll just keep growing. In August 2020 Gumtree reported that the value of the second-hand market rose by $3 billion to $46 billion. If it could rise that much when people were in lockdown, imagine how much it will grow with cost-of-living pressures increasing.

The second-hand economy is being driven by many things: the imperative to be more sustainable, the availability of technology that makes online buying and selling convenient, a desire to make cash while decluttering at home, to name just a few. I love the trend of people selling what they no longer need so much that I was inspired to create The Joyful Fashionista, an online marketplace buying and selling second-hand fashion items.

So, how much can you earn by selling stuff around your home? It depends on the item, the price and the demand. That last part is key. You never know whether someone wants an item until you list it, so why not give it a go? You might be surprised what people are looking for and what they're willing to pay for it. In my experience, not all items sell straight away; you need patience and sometimes to be prepared to reduce the price. Good photographs help, and this is increasingly easy to achieve with a smartphone.

While anyone can earn some quick cash from selling what they've got lying around the house, more and more people are turning both buying *and* selling into a lucrative business. Op shops, for instance, are now regularly combed by people looking for high-end brands or quirky retro looks to resell online. Over time you will develop good subject-matter expertise that could enable you to find bargains at garage sales or second-hand stores that you can then turn a bit of a profit on, be that at in-person at markets or at shopfront resellers, or online with platforms like Etsy, Depop and Shopify. With some commitment, you can develop a reputation and become a seller of choice.

Restore furniture

Furniture is often given away for free – or discarded – when people move or want to redecorate. In my Buy Nothing Project group, there are always sofas and bookcases being given away at the end of the year as people finish their studies and move away. I'm amazed by the amount of quality furniture that gets thrown out. While older pieces might look dated, their quality is often exceptional. With a bit of styling and some simple restoration work, you can update old furniture to make it look new again – and even make it pay.

My stepdaughter Sarah moved into her dream home last year and has been decorating with old furniture that she gave a new shabby-chic look to using pale-blue chalk paint. If chalk paint isn't your cup of tea, there are many other paints to choose from. She also likes to change handles to give her rescued furniture and other items a contemporary update. If you enjoy sewing, changing the upholstery is another a great way to restore furniture. Mid-century furniture, especially armchairs and lounge suites, are now highly prized – but the fabric needs updating.

You can find super easy tutorials on YouTube for guidance and inspiration on all of these restoration projects. While Sarah restores furniture for her home, there is always a market for fashionable furniture. Often people can't see the quality and beauty of design until a piece has been repainted or updated, and that disconnect is where you can make a bit of extra money that can end up making a real difference to your mortgage.

Get paid for tasks you enjoy

With so many people juggling dual careers, children and other caring responsibilities, there's little time for things like ironing – and many people simply hate doing it.

That's great news for those who love it, like my frugal friend Trish. When her children were teenagers Trish earned some extra cash by taking in ironing. She even invested in a specialised ironing press to ensure that tea towels had perfect edges. All her clients were local, and she built such a solid reputation that she attracted new clients through word of mouth and didn't have to do much advertising. She used her pocket money from ironing not to pay off her mortgage but for treats.

'I paid for skiing equipment, and for a skiing holiday away with the girls,' she said.

Online platforms such as Airtasker and Gumtree now make it easy to advertise your services. Costs vary, but a professional ironing service can charge between $25 and $30 per hour. The best part of this is that it's something you could do for an hour or two of an evening while watching a movie, or listening to a podcast or your favourite music.

Summary

- Having your own home means more space of your own – and not having to ask parents or housemates for permission to monetise extra space or use it as a base for a side hustle.

- The extra cash you earn can be used to reduce your mortgage fast.

- Plenty of people have unused space they could be making money from. Here are some ideas:
  - getting in a flatmate or housemate
  - becoming an Airbnb host
  - hosting students through a homestay arrangement
  - renting out a spare carspace.

- Side hustles (micro-businesses that you can carry out on the side of your central business) can help you to generate money from doing something you love. They may even become a main hustle. Some examples of side hustles I've seen in action include:
  - growing and selling excess fruit and vegetables
  - creating and selling arts and crafts made at home
  - breeding pets
  - selling second-hand items
  - restoring furniture
  - carrying out tasks like ironing.

There are so many ways to make a little extra money for your mortgage – often with little additional effort. Plus, we know that every extra dollar helps you reduce both how long it takes to pay your mortgage off and much you spend on interest. Next I'm going to share some tips on renovating as a home owner with a mortgage and show you how you can spruce up your space for less.

Chapter 14

Reimagining renos

When you purchase a home, especially if it's your first, spending money upfront to renovate and make your new nest look amazing is always tempting. You're likely to have people over, you might even plan a big housewarming party, and you *definitely* want your new home to look good. The things is, renovations aren't cheap – and they can really set you back when it comes to paying off your mortgage.

In this chapter I'm going to help you work through ways of balancing the natural desire to renovate with getting ahead on your mortgage. Renovations aren't off the table, I promise. However, it's important that you approach them strategically and with caution. I've also got plenty of tips for making your money stretch that bit further. Depending on the size of the renovations, what you can get for free or cheaply and how well you practise delayed gratification, the savings could fall anywhere between a few thousand dollars and $500,000.

Don't jump in right away

I know I said renovations aren't off the table, but before you take the credit card out on a tour of IKEA or Bunnings, stop and ask yourself if you really need that pizza oven, fire pit, movie theatre, landscaped garden and sleek kitchen with brand-name stainless steel appliances just yet. Of course, if your home is unsafe, uninsulated or extremely impracticable (for instance, it doesn't have a working bathroom or kitchen), you may need to renovate upfront. However, if it's not urgent, wait a while.

As I demonstrated in the first part of this book, the sooner you start smashing your mortgage, the more you will save in the long run. Delaying cosmetic renovations and instead paying down your mortgage will pay dividends – even if you feel like you can't quite see it yet.

In my experience, there are often additional advantages to waiting to get stuck into renovations. I think you need to live in a property for a full year before you can fully understand its advantages and disadvantages. You'll probably discover things in the garden that will sprout, flower and grow at different times – you might even discover bulbs you didn't know about. Those retro pink tiles in the bathroom might even become fashionable again, along with the Laura Ashley wallpaper. And things you don't necessarily like the look of might reveal themselves to be strategic choices to provide shade in summer or warmth in winter that you'll want to retain.

Do it yourself

You can save a small fortune by doing your own renovations. It's a lot of work, and it is usually harder, takes longer and costs more than you anticipate. However, overall, you definitely save more by doing it yourself. It also means that you know the quality of the work in your home, and you are engaged and connected with it.

These days, YouTube makes it easy for you to learn how to do almost anything. The Bunnings YouTube channel in particular has lots of helpful information. Bunnings also offers free in-person DIY workshops, and there are also courses available for purchase on renovation and building topics. If you are planning to eventually conduct an extensive renovation, which may include managing tradespeople, you might consider project management courses that are specific to construction. It might be an investment that saves you tens of thousands of dollars.

I asked Neil for his advice on this chapter as he's quite handy and regularly fixes things at home and in our investment properties. His biggest piece of advice is to not be scared to experiment.

'Try things in one room first,' he says. 'This will help get your skills up. Once you are more confident, you can try bigger projects.'

Spruce up your fugly interior

Sometimes, though aspects of your property might be functional, they might look a little, um, fugly. Before you rip something out and replace it, consider whether you can extend its life with some minor changes. You may even find that some minor updates that were intended to be temporary look so good they become permanent. Here is a selection of some of my favourite ways of jazzing up some tired-looking interiors without spending loads of money:

· **Remove carpet stains.** Before you rip up the carpet and replace it with something new, remove the most offensive stains. You could have your carpet professionally cleaned, but in my experience they don't always get rid of the worst stains. I purchased a Bissell Little Green® Portable Spot & Stain Carpet Cleaner several years ago, and it's done a great job of cleaning up stains left by my kids. It's even helped to remove some hardy grease stains on the carpet at an investment property.

- **Paint over wacky tiles.** Have you got tiles that may be retro but will never be cool? If they aren't chipped or broken, you can paint over them. White Knight produces a range of tile and laminate paints that can do the trick. It's important to follow the directions and do the appropriate preparation, especially if the tiles are in a wet area, such as a shower. Honestly, this is so transformative. I once painted old tiles in a bright kitchen yellow. While we replaced the kitchen a few years after that with an open plan and newer look, those bright yellow tiles caught the light and brought me so much joy whenever I walked in.

- **Paint or cover over benchtops.** I don't know why burnt orange benchtops were ever a thing, but they were and now they definitely aren't. A kitchen is often the heart of a home and somewhere you're likely to spend a lot of time. Rather than spending tens of thousands of dollars installing a new kitchen, you can update a benchtop by simply painting it. You need specialist paints suitable for a laminated surface, but the good news is that it is achievable, and there are YouTube tutorials (including a couple from Bunnings) to help. You can also buy adhesive vinyl, often known as 'contact', made to cover over benchtops in designs including wood and marble effect. While there are some limitations to vinyl (for example, you can't put hot pots or pans on it), it's not too bad as a short-term fix.

- **Clean your walls and doors.** Before you go to the trouble of completely repainting a space, consider giving it a really thorough clean. If the paintwork isn't chipped, it might just need cleaning to remove accumulated dust or dirt. This is easy to do using warm water and liquid soap (and my orange miracle spray detailed in chapter 12 also works). Light scratches and scuffs can be removed using toothpaste and a slightly abrasive sponge (the green side on a yellow and green sponge, not steel wool).

- **Paint your furniture.** Older-style furniture, including built-in wardrobes, can be updated easily with paint. As I detailed in chapter 13, one of my stepdaughters turns old furniture into shabby-chic masterpieces using chalk paint. Her creations are beautiful. Paint companies now even have specialist products that allow you to create marble, metallic, distressed and concrete effects.

- **Change handles and fixtures.** It's often easier and cheaper to change outdated handles on a vanity, wardrobe or sink than to buy a whole new one. Little things like handles can make a big impact, and it's not difficult (or expensive) to change them.

- **Add peel-and-stick floor tiles.** Before you rip out and update a tiled floor, consider 'tiling' over with vinyl tiles. Some look so realistic you would swear they were real timber, stone or tiles. They also come in a range of patterns and designs, including some incredibly artistic ones. I used some recently to cover over old chipboard shelving, and I was surprised by how good it looked once installed.

Hire or borrow tools and equipment

My father-in-law has an impressive shed of tools, and we often borrow from him if we need to fix something around the apartment. Borrowing tools from friends and family is a great way to save money when you've got some work to do on your home. However, it's important to treat these tools with respect and return them in good condition. For many people, their tools are precious. Don't be careless with them.

You can also hire tools and equipment from commercial providers, which is especially useful when you need to use big or expensive equipment (for example, a Bobcat) for a short period of time. Bunnings has a hire facility, as do many Mitre 10 stores.

There are also specialist stores, such as Kennards Hire and Coates, as well as local providers to choose from.

Another way to get tools cheaply is to join a community library. Community Toolbox Canberra is a community-led and volunteer-run tool and equipment library. For an annual fee, you can borrow and use their wide range of tools and equipment. Whenever I check out their inventory, I'm like a kid in a candy store. They have everything from cooking items (think pressure canners, ice-cream machines and pasta makers) to jackhammers, air compressors, carpet cleaners and all sorts of drills and drill bits. What I really like about this initiative is that it makes it possible for apartment-dwelling people like me to have access to tools (and my favourites: kitchen gadgets and equipment). It also helps people to save money and encourages sustainability.

The sustainable online marketplace Rosella Street also facilitates renting (or buying) a range of items – including tools – cheaply and supports the circular economy.

Hold a renos party

How do you feel when a friend or family member purchases a new home? Do you feel excited and happy for them and want to help? You may turn up to a housewarming party with a houseplant or a Bunnings gift voucher, but what if you could help them instead?

Instead of a housewarming party, why not have a renos party? Housewarming parties are fun, but they can put pressure on new home owners for their place to live up to expectations. It takes a while to move, settle in, unpack, hang your artwork and do any essential renos.

What if, instead of waiting until your home is perfect, you invited people around to help? Invite people over to help with things like painting prep (washing down walls), painting, weeding, gardening, building retaining walls and general tidying up. Put on a BBQ or pizzas, and make it a bit of fun. You might be surprised who turns up to help and who has some great tips for renovating based on their experience.

Lauren Harkness took this approach when she turned an abandoned church into a venue and retreat space now called 'Sanctuary, Canberra'. When Lauren took possession of the church it was dated and dirty. She enlisted the help of several friends who came and helped over a few days. I spent a few hours washing up discoveries in the kitchen and cleaning out cupboards, while another friend cleaned the toilets. While it mightn't sound like fun, I felt like I was part of something; I was helping in a tangible way, meeting people and connecting. In just days we had transformed that abandoned church into a beautiful, stylish event space that was ready to host important events such as weddings.

Find mentors

When my ex-husband and I undertook extensive renovations on the former family home, I noticed how other men, especially recently retired men, enjoyed mentoring him through the process. They freely gave of their time and knowledge and often came over to help – sometimes spending nearly the entire day. We had neighbours from down the street, friends from his Rotary Club and work colleagues all help at various times with different projects. Never be scared to ask for help; people are often willing to share their time and expertise. There will often be a way that you can help them in the future, although sometimes your gift of friendship may be enough. That said, a slab of beer, some pizza, a meal out or a box of chocolates as a thank-you is always polite.

Sadly, in my experience, women don't tend to mentor other women in quite the same way. This is largely because, historically, women didn't learn the skills to do hands-on renovation work. Women also tend to be super busy, especially if they have children or grandchildren. It's easy to think that renovating is a blokey thing that only tradies can do, but women are tradies too – and even untrained women can be good at performing many hands-on renovation jobs. (If you can ice a cake, you can plaster.) The good news is that women renovation role models are becoming more visible (for example, Cherie Barber and Three Birds Renovations), and this is helping to break down stereotypes.

There are also more and more non-gendered resources for handy advice. Bunnings, for instance, has done work to ensure that its education, customer services and support are inclusive. If you watch its videos – and I recommend that you do because they can be very helpful for DIYers – you may notice that there is diversity in its breadth of educators.

Renovation involves many tasks that aren't just about power tools or technical know-how. A successful renovation requires skill sets such as interior design, planning, budgeting, project management, negotiating, procurement, contract management, cleaning and catering. Maybe 'all' you are doing is searching on the internet, choosing the colour scheme, washing down walls, sweeping, making lunches, shopping or vacuuming. But those are essential tasks, and you are doing a lot to contribute. Work together as a team and know that everyone's skills are important to achieving the overall vision.

Things you should never do

While you can learn to do many things through trial and error, there are certain things you should only ever get a qualified tradesperson to do. Be careful not to void your property insurance, and never attempt to do anything that is particularly complicated or dangerous. Here are some tips for things to avoid:

- Don't knock down walls yourself, even if you're pretty sure they aren't load-bearing. The risks of causing major structural damage to your home are too great.

- Never play around with electrical things, especially if you're renovating an old home. Pay for an electrician to ensure the job is done safely and properly. (For older premises, it's probably a good idea to get someone in to check the wiring is safe, even if you hadn't planned on making any changes – you just never know.)

- Unless you know exactly what you're doing, don't get up on a ladder, especially on a roof. Working on a ladder requires knowledge of safety procedures that many people skip. According to a Safe Work Australia report, falls from heights were the cause of 30 per cent of worker fatalities in Australia in 2019. People start to lose their balance at a certain age, and a ladder is not a good place for dads and granddads who still think they're in their 20s.

- Don't try to fix plumbing yourself. Thinking he could fix a minor leak in the hot water system of one of our investment properties, Neil replaced the culprit: a corroded valve. Unfortunately, weeping around the seal led to minor flooding. A replacement hot water system had to be installed by a plumber and, with the emergency call-out fee, it was an expensive bill.

Renovate with impact – and avoid overcapitalising

If you haven't watched a reality renovation show, where have you been? The contestants typically compete to create luxurious updates, and often with dazzling results – but do extensive renovations really add value?

As I was drafting this chapter, Neil told me about a three-bedroom house in suburban Queanbeyan that had undergone a major renovation. Among many other changes, the garage had become a man cave with a bar. After months of renovation, the property was passed in at auction. The cooling property market was partly to blame, but it is also likely that they overcapitalised. At the end of the day, it was still a three-bedroom house with no ensuite in a comfortable but not prime suburb, and it was never going to reach a large price.

Conventional wisdom is that to successfully renovate you need to buy the worst house in the best street and then do it up. Renovating for impact is a bit more involved, but you do have to be wary about spending more on renovations than you will get back. You may be installing things for lifestyle, and that's fine if it's what you want to enjoy. However, if you need to sell your home one day, it's good to know you what kind of value you will get back.

There are plenty of renovations that that can add value to your home. Here are some popular examples:

- **A secure garage.** People love their cars, and those who work in trades may have expensive tools in their cars that they want locked up. Many people will pay a premium for a home with a good-quality garage.

- **Decks or pergolas.** Good outside areas enhance liveability and extend the floor space of your home. However, it's important to ensure that any such renovations are safe and approved.

- **Curb appeal.** Focusing on making the outside of your home look attractive will help with the value. What do people see first when searching for a home? The outside. First impressions are important; some potential buyers might not even go into a house if what they see from the curb is unappealing, so focus on making the front garden neat and presentable, ensuring the front door looks great and that there is no junk or mess hanging around.

- **Energy efficiency upgrades.** Installing things like solar panels on the roof can help you save money on electricity in the long run, but it can also increase the value of your home. People are increasingly valuing sustainability, and energy efficiency measures are likely to be seen positively by prospective buyers.

In contrast, some renovations can actually detract from the value of your home. Here are some examples of renovations to be wary of:

- **Swimming pools.** You may love a swimming pool, but not everyone wants to maintain one. In a cooler climate where you can only swim for a few months of the year, having a pool may be more trouble than it's worth – particularly if you factor heating into the running cost. Install a swimming pool for lifestyle if you want, but ensure you put in a good regulation fence and don't bank on a sizable return.

- **Larger rooms.** Sometimes people choose to bring down walls in a home to create a parents' retreat or gym, or to open the main living space. The problem with this is that it tends to reduce the number of bedrooms in a property. A five-bedroom house becomes a four-bedroom house, and when it's listed on the market it needs to compete with four- rather than five-bedroom houses.

- **Expensive kitchens.** If you remove a functioning kitchen for the sake of installing a shiny new kitchen, be aware that it might not add the value you expect.

- **Unapproved structures.** No matter how nice a new improvement looks, it will impact the sale price if it's not an approved structure. Depending on what it is, there may be more severe economic consequences. For example, if someone makes a complaint about an unapproved structure, you may end up with a fine and having to remove the work altogether. Stick with the regulations, and when in doubt, don't.

- **Adding an additional storey.** Building an additional storey is usually an expensive thing to do. It can work, and I've seen it work, but homes generally aren't designed to have an additional floor stacked on top. (If you think about it, they usually have sloping roofs, for one thing.) Sometimes it can be cheaper to knock down and rebuild a much larger structure.

Again, before embarking on any renovations, decide whether they are essential right now or can wait until your mortgage is more manageable.

Remember: keep it simple and classic

In the late 1980s I lived in a home with pink walls and thick cornflower-blue carpet. I loved it, but not everyone did, and it didn't date well. These days, when I renovate, I generally keep it simple. Antique White U.S.A® – a warm white that's slightly creamier and less stark than pure white – is now my go-to colour. It's a neutral backdrop that can be paired with artwork, furniture and curtains or other fittings, especially those in blue, green and copper tones. I've been choosing that colour for over 20 years now, and it hasn't dated in that time (unlike mission brown and burnt orange). If you're reading this book in 2043, stop by and tell me if a basic white is still in fashion – I'd be surprised if it was on the nose.

The bottom line is this: choose simple, especially if you plan to resell. You might love the quirkiness of a retro-inspired kitchen, but will potential buyers love it the way you do?

Summary

· Delay major renovations for as long as possible and focus instead on getting ahead in your mortgage payments. With the power of compound interest, this can end up saving you a lot of money.

· If and when you do decide to renovate, keep it classic and low-cost wherever possible.

· Learning how to DIY and borrowing or hiring tools are good ways of saving money, but be aware of undertaking dangerous work yourself.

· Invite people over for a renos party rather than a housewarming party and seek out renovation mentors. You might be surprised what you learn.

· Before spending big, make sure your renovations are adding value to your home in the long run.

In part II I've covered all sorts of ways of saving money, rounding off with this chapter on making your new home look and feel good without laying down money that's better spent on paying your mortgage off. Next I'm going to talk through navigating life while paying a mortgage off – the good and the bad – and what comes after.

PART III

LIFE
HAPPENS

Chapter 15

Give me a break

You might be asking yourself if, with all of the saving and hard work of paying your mortgage off, you can ever have fun.

Well, the good news is, yes! You *can* still have fun while paying off your mortgage, but it does require setting a budget, planning and a mindset shift. In this chapter I'll walk you through what it means to travel while prioritising your mortgage and share some tips for helping you stretch your money further if you do decide to get away.

Balance your priorities

I still managed some travel while paying off my mortgage, but it wasn't the priority. I remember, years ago, spending a Saturday night at home sipping port and listening to Neil Diamond music – on a cassette – while playing Scrabble. That might not sound so exciting, particularly if you're dreaming of an overseas adventure, but I look back fondly on that time. It helped me achieve my financial goals. And I still enjoy Neil Diamond.

I've talked about priorities and delayed gratification a few times in this book, and the concepts are relevant again here. Yes, you can travel and have fun while chipping away at your mortgage, but you're kidding yourself if you think you can have expensive overseas trips and, at the same time, pay your mortgage off quickly without making any changes. The key is, as always, to figure out your priorities, do your maths and then act in ways that help you meet your goals. You may find you can make changes that allow you to travel and stay ahead of your mortgage. But you may instead decide to delay gratification and enjoy cosy evenings at home. After all, you'll be in a much better position to afford that expensive trip when you're mortgage free.

After Neil and I got engaged, we sat down, set out our goals and made a joint budget. We knew that in that calendar year we planned to get married, go on a family honeymoon cruise from Singapore back to Australia, and travel – I had a work trip to Europe, and Neil wanted to come along with me. We were also in the process of buying investment properties. I tallied up our joint incomes, fixed expenses and what we planned to do, and I found that (funnily enough) I wouldn't be able to pay off my mortgage at the speed I wanted. So, I went into action. We rented out a spare room. We also set a budget of $5000 for our wedding (we ended up spending just over $4000 for 200 guests). This all meant that I was able to meet my mortgage-payment goals *and* enjoy travel with my family.

Ignore FOMO

If you look at social media, it seems like the whole world is out there having fun – except you. However, a photo or video captures only a point in time, and it doesn't paint a complete picture of what's going on in someone's life. You don't know if they were really enjoying themselves or not. For example, even when I was experiencing domestic violence, I wanted to portray the positives; however, under the surface, our happy family times were usually less than happy.

I'm editing this book while on a cruise in the Pacific with family. I'm sending out photos of us snorkelling in crystal-clear waters and drinking from green coconuts. What I'm not showing are the days when a large swell is making us feel queasy. And while it's an awesome cruise, on any given day there are many people onboard who aren't happy about things: the food, the entertainment, their cocktails – whatever.

The moral here is never to compare yourself with others and what they're doing or not doing. The fact that friends and acquaintances seem to be travelling a lot and enjoying themselves doesn't mean anything. It's their journey; you don't know if they're in debt or arguing the whole time. You will probably never know. One thing I *do* know is that staying in your own lane and focusing on achieving your own goals leads to satisfaction and accomplishment. Maybe staying at home listening to Neil Diamond isn't your thing. However, by choosing frugal entertainment and perhaps delaying that dream holiday, you'll sleep better knowing that you're prioritising your long-term financial wellbeing over short-term fun.

Set money aside for travel

For many years Neil and I didn't have a travel budget. I regret that we didn't, as it meant that I often stressed about spending money on holidays – not just about the outlay itself, but also about having no clear boundaries to the total spend. Having paid off my mortgage, we now set aside $300 each pay period into a separate bank account (more on this in chapter 17). Factoring in interest, this amounts to about $8000 a year. We make this stretch with some of the travel hacks I share later in this chapter.

You could easily put money for separate expenses, such as travel, into separate accounts. However, the dilemma you have as a mortgage holder is that you would then forgo the interest benefits of putting this money on your mortgage. Plus, you will pay tax on the interest earnt. Instead, I suggest you set an annual travel budget. You continue to pay as much as you can onto your mortgage, but you redraw as required for travel. You can track your travel planning in an Excel spreadsheet. This is messier than having a separate account, but you benefit from the tax-free interest savings.

Don't feel guilty about using the money you've budgeted and set aside for travel. You've allocated this money for a reason. You might go crazy if you don't holiday! If you have children, you'll probably want to spend some quality time with them while they're young. If you don't, this doesn't mean no holidays – or, on the flipside, expensive holidays. You don't need to spend lots of money to connect, but you do need to look at your priorities and be intentional with your time and money. If you're planning a family, there are also benefits to travelling before you have kids, especially if you dream of backpacking overseas!

Stay close to home

The Chinese philosopher Zhuangzi (aka Chuang-Tzu) said that when you have reached a certain understanding of the world, you can see it from the comfort of your own room. I like my room, but I also like going out of it to explore. However, Zhuangzi has a point in that travel is about seeing the physical world from a different perspective, and doing that is about mindset rather than physical reality. So, if you're prioritising your mortgage and have limited funds for travel, before you go overseas, why not enjoy what you have around you?

Several years ago I was chosen to participate in Visit Canberra's 101 Local Humans campaign, which used local bloggers, photographers and social media gurus to promote Canberra as a tourist destination. What was special about my year as a 'human' was how I connected with the local environment on a deeper level. I even got to enjoy a bespoke experience at the National Portrait Gallery with my children and my sister's family. So many people come to Canberra, see Parliament House at Capital Hill and then go home, but there's so much more to see! Entry to many national institutions, for example, is free. I can stand in front of Jackson Pollock's famous *Blue Poles*, valued at half a billion dollars, for free! (Speaking from experience though, it's important to be careful not to stand too close to avoid setting off the alarm.) What amazing collections or experiences where you live are free or very cheap?

Do some research on where you can go on day trips or long weekends that are close to home. I'm not suggesting you never go overseas, just that you stop and enjoy where you are first: the beauty of changing autumn leaves, fresh air on mountain hikes, swimming at the beach, viewing a travelling art exhibition, or lighting up a fire pit and inviting friends to join you under the stars.

Accommodation

One of the most expensive parts of travel is accommodation, so it's a good place to start when thinking about ways to make travel more affordable while paying your mortgage off. Here are some accommodation hacks for spending less when travelling.

Staying with friends

Neil and I have good friends who live in Tathra on the NSW south coast, and we visit them regularly. We go for walks down to the beach and back, and explore local areas such as the heritage-listed Tathra Wharf. Neil drinks beer, plays darts and talks a lot of rot with Alan, while Helen and I cook, drink prosecco, play rummy or go shopping. Helen loves putting up Christmas and Halloween decorations and spoiling my boys with homemade milkshakes and pancakes. We still do things we want to do independently (I may or may not have gotten lost in the local op shop for 90 minutes), but mostly we go there to spend time with our friends. A secondary benefit, of course, is that it's frugal.

It's essential, as a guest, to be careful about not overstaying your welcome. I was asked on ABC local radio once whether staying with friends is a good way to save money. I laughingly answered that it's an affordable way to travel – provided you're a welcome guest and not a freeloader! There's nothing worse than feeling that your friendship exists only for free accommodation, or that you're being taken for granted, so be mindful of your hosts. We always take food and drinks to share, though Helen often finds creative ways to package it up for us to take home again without us realising it. We sometimes also take DVDs to watch, but we generally find entertainment enough in each other's company.

Camping and caravanning

Camping is a bit of an Australian tradition, and it's a great way to see the great outdoors without spending much money. When they were young, my kids often preferred this accommodation to a hotel room – especially if there was somewhere to swim nearby. Having their own tent gave them independence, and they loved having the space to run around and be with other kids. Caravanning is also a great way to travel reasonably inexpensively (if you already have a caravan or can rent or borrow one from a friend).

Campsites and caravan parks are usually pretty inexpensive, and you can even camp for free in some places, with some local council areas, clubs and pubs offering free sites to encourage visitors. The WikiCamps Australia app offers a guide to both free and paid sites around the country. Caravan parks also often have happy hours where people can mingle, and there are plenty of blogs filled with hacks about cooking and living frugally on the road.

Putting aside picking a place to pitch your tent, camping – and caravanning – has to come with a frugality warning. Anyone who has ever set foot in lifestyle stores such as BCF knows you can spend a fortune on all sorts of stuff, and plenty of people end up purchasing equipment they never use – be honest here, are you one of them? Before you buy, ask a friend if you can borrow their gear. (Make sure to return it in good condition and give them a small gift, such as a box of chocolates, to say thank you.) You can also often get some basic equipment by asking in your local Buy Nothing Project group.

Want the feeling of a holiday without going anywhere? Pitching a tent in the backyard gives you an opportunity to test your equipment and see if you have what you need before you go anywhere, and it can be a good experience of independence for teen or tween children.

Home exchange

What if you could swap homes with someone else? Home exchange, or house swapping, has been around for a while. Pre-COVID, it experienced a boom in popularity due to the ease of setting up arrangements online through platforms including HomeExchange, Love Home Swap and HomeLink. The idea is simple: you go on holiday and stay in someone else's home. Meanwhile, they come and stay in your home. Things like private vehicles can also be included in the exchange, and there are even specialist categories for exchangers and the homes they offer, such as Rotarians, people over 50 and luxury.

Trish, who you'll be familiar with by now, and her husband Bob have spent many years travelling the globe since their retirement, and that includes six years of not living in their home. Much of this was made possible through home exchanges. Trish joined HomeLink online and, after paying the annual fee, gained access to other listed members. Though she could have joined as a visitor to avoid the fee, she opted to pay what is no more than the cost of one night's accommodation in an inner-city hotel for additional protection and access to a dedicated helpline.

I've watched Trish and Bob go on home exchange and prepare for visitors for many years now. Trish enjoys chatting with potential exchanges and prepares detailed information for them for when they arrive. While they don't typically meet face to face, she often forms friendships with guests on exchange. In return for their hospitality, Trish and Bob have also been welcomed into people's homes and communities. To them, home exchange is a way of being part of a global community.

House-sitting

Another way to get a change of scene is to house-sit while a household is away on an extended holiday or work placement. There is often no charge for this if you are prepared to look after the pets and keep the garden tidy. You don't even have to go far to benefit from a change of scene. If you live in the inner city, for example, you might find a house-sitting gig near the water or in the hills.

Several websites, such as TrustedHousesitters, House Carers and Mindahome, connect homeowners with house-sitters. You can also join Facebook groups (search for House Sitting World, Aussie House Sitters, House Sitting Australia and Pet Sitting Australia) to connect with other house-sitters and find out about upcoming opportunities.

Couch surfing

In 2015, Sarah and Laura from Keepin' It Frugal quit their jobs, sold their possessions and travelled around the world for a year before returning to South Australia. Their travels took them to Singapore, Japan and Taiwan, then to Europe, Indonesia and back to Australia. All up, they spent $32,000 on a fantastic year of travel that they will never forget. One of the ways they were able to travel so affordably was couch surfing. They signed up at couchsurfing.com, searched for where they wanted to go and what they wanted to do, and read the hosts' profiles. Being foodies, they had a strong interest in food and culture, so they looked specifically for people who were well travelled or also loved food. They would send hosts a message to say they wanted to 'cook surf' rather than 'couch surf'. Then, while staying at their place, they would cook a dish from their country, and their hosts would cook a dish from theirs.

Sarah said that one of the best parts of the couch surfing experience was the sort of connection it encouraged between hosts and guests.

'One of the biggest differences between Airbnb and couch surfing is that you do spend a lot more time with the host,' she said. 'You know you might end up going out together for lunches and dinners and spending a lot more time with them, whereas sometimes with Airbnb it's just expected that you stay in the room and they're either not there at all or it's very minimal contact.'

Timeshare

On a recent trip to the USA, Neil and I were 'encouraged' to attend a timeshare presentation. We were promised it would be over in two hours, but we struggled to get out of there in under three. Always be careful when someone forces you to endure sales spruiking.

Timeshare schemes are more sophisticated than they were in the past, with a wide range of properties available. In essence, what they are selling is a long-term commitment (plus a one-off deposit fee) that includes an annual fee plus maintenance; you then receive points that you can redeem at various locations.

I've crunched the numbers, and what they are selling is reasonable – but only if you can afford to pay it. It's not reasonable if you buy it on credit, nor when you consider the opportunity cost of not paying the same money on your mortgage or investing it elsewhere. Consider any arrangement carefully, as it will create a long-term commitment and can result in a loss of flexibility. Never commit under pressure, and always do your sums carefully.

Airbnb

Though it was inspired by an air mattress on the floor, Airbnb now includes luxurious stays. In fact, it's often easier to book luxury accommodation on Airbnb than the cheaper stuff!

As I mentioned in an earlier chapter, Neil and I have been Airbnb hosts in the past, and we've had plenty of good experiences. However, there are a few things to watch out for as a guest. First, you must be clear about whether the accommodation is shared with the owners (or others) or whether it is yours alone for the duration of your stay. You'll also need to watch those cleaning fees. Additionally, you need to be aware of fraudulent home hosts. Always read the reviews carefully, and when in doubt, stay with someone who has Superhost credentials.

All things considered, it's sometimes more comfortable to choose a hotel. The title of an article by Arwa Mahdawi in *The Guardian* says it all, really: 'Airbnb feels like staying with a cheap, uptight friend – then paying for the privilege'. We still enjoy staying at Airbnbs, especially as it often provides more comforts than a hotel; however, we're increasingly finding good value at reasonably priced hotel and motel chains, especially if they have loyalty programs.

Hotel loyalty programs

The Guardian article I referred to a moment ago references a viral tweet by writer Jeremy Gordon: 'Decided to stay in a Holiday Inn instead of an Airbnb for an overnight trip and strongly feel, one hour after check-in, that there has never been a more luxurious experience in all of human history'.

I relate to that tweet because Neil and I often stay at Holiday Inn and other hotels within the IHG Hotels & Resorts network. As a member of the network, Neil accumulates points that he can redeem for free accommodation, and he's often upgraded and always treated well. For example, on a recent trip to the USA we spent four nights at Holiday Inn Express – all made possible by points. While it wasn't glamorous, it was clean, comfortable and included breakfast. I actually preferred our Holiday Inn stay to the more luxurious accommodation we had earlier in the trip. Maybe it's my inner frugalista, but I felt more comfortable at the Holiday Inn and found the staff and other guests easy to talk to. I also didn't have to worry about being upsold or having to give out lavish tips.

Frequent flyer and other points programs

Neil and I did much of our travel to the USA for #FinCon22 – including visits to the Kennedy Space Center, Key Largo and Miami Beach – using points we had accumulated as Qantas Frequent Flyers and through hotel loyalty schemes. The way these programs tend to work is that you accumulate points for certain actions, such as flying with a particular airline or making purchases using a program-specific card, and then cash those points in on what's offered by your program. As travel is important to us, and we saw good value in the conversion offered, Neil and I chose to spend those points on seeing the world.

Though it can be tempting, it generally isn't good value to purchase points directly – unless there's a special promotion. In preparation for booking accommodation recently, Neil calculated that 1 Qantas Point has the purchasing power of roughly 1 cent. He then used points to secure ten nights' accommodation for 156,000 Qantas Points, having already searched through comparison websites to establish the cash price would have been around $1500. Had he not had the points already and decided to purchase the same number of points directly through Qantas, it would have cost him $4000 dollars.

Furthermore, buying something just for the points is never good value. If you're planning to buy something anyway, the points are like the cherry on top. For instance, if you planned to buy an air fryer, it's best to search for the lowest price; but if the store with the best price happened to offer points, that's an added bonus. Understanding that your purchasing decisions should never be driven purely by points is particularly important when considering essential purchases such as groceries, as people often shop at a more expensive stores for loyalty schemes that offer points. However, if you're paying $50 more for 50 cents of value, you're actually paying $49.50 *more* overall. Always do your sums before making purchases, especially significant purchases, and treat points as a nice bonus.

Transport

Getting to and then around your destination is the other significant expense of holidays. However, with some creative thinking and research, you can make big savings. Here are my top tips.

Flights

Travel search engine sites such as Skyscanner, KAYAK and Expedia can make it easier to compare flights and get a bargain. Make sure to book through sites that you consider reliable.

We increasingly choose to book flights directly with an airline, usually those we know and like. We sign up for newsletters and connect on social media, note when things are on sale and book when we know we are planning to travel somewhere. It pays to do your research, compare deals and book in advance.

As with accommodation, points programs can also be useful when booking airfares. Much as we do when using cash, we try to maximise the buying power of our points by booking travel during sales, and this is made easier with the protection our Qantas Frequent Flyer memberships give us. We used points to book our flights to the USA around a year before leaving and got a good deal. We were able to book so far ahead without too much worry because we knew that using Qantas Points meant there would be no cancellation or booking-change fees if we needed to cancel or change our flights. (The pandemic taught us a lot about how plans can change suddenly.) Be sure to check the details of your program, of course, but when we've had to change flights booked with Qantas Points previously due to COVID-19 travel restrictions, the points were refunded and back in our account within 24 hours.

Finally, it pays to pack light. Cheap fares on budget airlines often come with conditions, one of which is baggage allowance. If your ticket states you can only take 7 kg of carry-on and one piece of checked luggage that weighs 23 kg, the airline will likely charge you if you go over this amount. Small travel scales are available cheaply and are a good investment if you are travelling with a budget airline or on a heavily discounted fare.

Trains

I love train travel, and in some countries it's an essential part of the experience. When we lived in Taiwan, I used to take my kids for rides on the MRT (subway) just for fun. Taiwan also has high-speed rail, old-fashioned trains that venture into the hills and a train service along the spectacular east coast where mountains crash down to the sea.

In addition to the magic you might not otherwise get to access, rail travel is also often cheaper than air travel or hire cars. Some destinations have travel passes that allow unrestricted travel in certain areas. For instance, travellers to Japan might find that purchasing the Japan Rail Pass, which covers travel for up to three weeks, may prove to be good value for money. Recently, we travelled by train to Sydney to connect with our cruise and noticed that the fares had been reduced due to government support; my sons travelled with us for only $1 each!

The road trip

Are we there yet? What would an Aussie holiday be without a good old-fashioned road trip. My husband was reminiscing recently about road trips when he was thrown in the back of the family station wagon to separate him from his three sisters. Oh, the days before safety regulations! I'm always surprised there aren't more Australian movies about road trips, as they are part of our shared experience. We have *Charlie & Boots*, *Last Cab to Darwin* and *The Adventures of Priscilla, Queen of the Desert* but not as many more as you might expect.

I like to treat road travel as being just as much a part of the experience as the destination. So, with a good playlist or a podcast or two to listen to, and the kids in the back with pillows, the open road awaits. I often have some of my best aha moments while driving longer distances, as being in the car gives me more space for thinking.

My friend and organising and decluttering coach Lauren Winzar pulled off possibly one of the best family holidays ever: a road trip to the Australian Dinosaur Trail in outback Queensland. Lauren's daughter has a fascination for dinosaurs, so they took a trip through the outback, dodging floods, before heading back down the Queensland coast and home to Canberra. What I loved about this is that they decided what they wanted to do as a family, including visiting a working drive-in cinema, having a family playlist and spending time on the coast.

Public transport

I enjoy using public transport when travelling overseas. It allows me to meet people and see things at a leisurely pace. It's ideal when you're on holiday as you're not likely to be rushed for time.

My frugal friend Trish has good advice regarding public transport on holiday: 'Use public transport wherever and whenever possible. However, it's not worth lugging suitcases along a hot pavement to get onto a crowded bus to pay a minimum fare instead of catching a shuttle or taxi for a little more cost but triple the comfort.'

Walking

I like to walk wherever possible on holidays. Not only does it enable me to observe things in my local area in a more accessible way, but it also helps me stretch my legs after spending so long sitting during travel.

Tourism offices in many towns and cities have cultural or heritage walking trail maps for visitors, often with explanations about places of interest. These can be great self-paced tours for getting your bearings while also learning something. My favourite of these has to be Battery Point in Hobart as it includes a vintage store *and* a bakery.

While walking in a new place is a frugal and sustainable way to get around, it's not always possible to do so safely, so getting local advice is important. When we were in Florida, Neil and I originally planned to walk the 20 minutes from our hotel to the conference venue. However, there was no sidewalk (footpath) for most of the way. When we did a trial walk, we found that motorists tended to come too close to the side of the road for our comfort and there were a lot of honking horns. In addition, as it was hot and stormy, the grass was long, and signs at our hotel warned about snakes and alligators, so we didn't feel safe.

Money

Thinking about money and how you'll access it in the currency you need is an important thing to do before you leave for an overseas trip. Will you be using cash all the time, as we did on our cruise to the Pacific Islands? Or is your destination somewhere like the USA or New Zealand, where Neil and I found we almost always used our cards? Either way, avoid getting hit by unexpected conversion or transaction fees by choosing a card with low or no charges for international purchases. Some examples include the Bankwest Zero Mastercard and Latitude 28° Global Platinum Mastercard. Some banks, such as ING and HSBC, have accounts with global wallets that allow you to lock in exchange rates and withdraw cash in local currency with no transaction fees from certain ATMs.

Communications

One of the frustrating things about travelling overseas is not being able to make phone calls or connect to the internet easily. You can prepare for this by purchasing a local sim card for the region you're going to travel in, either from Amazon or direct from the supplier (often you can pick it up at the airport for no extra charge), before you leave. We did this for recent travel to the USA (T-Mobile) and New Zealand (One NZ) and found it worked well. Beyond being able to call ahead for accommodation or other reservations, it allowed us access to the internet so we could use Google Maps and even book Ubers to get around more easily.

Summary

- It might feel like everyone else in the world is having adventures except for you, but stick with your goals and live within your finances.

- Decide what you want to spend on travel and budget accordingly.

- Enjoy the beauty and hidden treasures of where you live before travelling further. It's usually a lot cheaper than the alternative, and you might be surprised by what you find.

- There are many ways to save on accommodation costs, including home exchange, camping and loyalty programs.

- Points programs can be useful for affordable holidays, but avoid spending just to collect points.

- You can save money on transport by booking flights when on sale, walking or taking public transport where possible, investing in rail passes and choosing a good old-fashioned Aussie adventure (a road trip).

If you've just bought a home, it mightn't be the time to jet off on a luxury holiday, but you can still travel while getting ahead on your mortgage with a bit of compromise and some handy hacks. Though it's so much fun to plan for things like holidays, what do you do when things go wrong? In the next chapter I'll help you prepare for scenarios that no-one wants to live through but everyone should be ready for.

Chapter 16

When shit happens

Life rarely goes to plan. When most people buy a home, they dream about their future life in their forever home. But things can happen. Someone might lose their job in an economic downturn. They might get divorced, or have twins, or discover their partner has a gambling addiction. Or maybe interest rates go up and they find out they've overextended. Any of these scenarios can lead to financial difficulty.

According to the Australian Financial Complaints Authority (AFCA; more about them later in this chapter), financial difficulty occurs when someone is temporarily unable to make repayments on their loans. This can be caused by things such as sickness, over-commitment, business downturn, separation, unexpected medical or funeral expenses, reduction in work hours and events such as natural disasters.

Whether it's your 'fault' or not, shit happens – and often it's unforeseen. But if it does happen, either to you or to someone you know, this chapter contains some advice on how to get through it.

Financial difficulty and the brain

If you've ever been through any financial difficulty, you know it can be stressful and overwhelming. It can even lead to problems sleeping and making decisions. What you might not know is that it makes people less intelligent, at least for a while.

According to a 2013 study, people struggling with debt or financial stress temporarily lose around 13 IQ points. As Harvard economist and the study's co-author Sendhil Mullainathan explains, being focused on unpaid mortgages and bills affects our ability to think about other things.

'When we think about people who are financially stressed, we think they are short on money, but the truth is they are also short on cognitive capacity,' he said.

In this study, when people with incomes of about US$70,000 and people with incomes of about US$20,000 were presented with a small hypothetical car bill, they scored reasonably evenly on cognitive testing. However, when asked to consider a much larger bill, study participants with lower incomes experienced a 40 per cent drop in cognitive capacity that wasn't mirrored by those with higher incomes. The study also tested farmers in India who were paid just once a year with the harvest. The difference in their IQ scores before the harvest – before their once-yearly payment, when they are under the greatest financial stress – was 25 per cent lower than after they had been paid. What this suggests is that people going through financial hardship and stress experience a drop in cognitive capacity, which negatively affects their ability to find solutions to debt problems.

The sense of dread and doom that comes with financial hardship flows into other aspects of life. According to Nicole Flaws, formerly a counsellor at the financial counselling organisation Care, it can be hard to separate a financial issue from other issues.

'It's hugely emotional and can impact your mental health and also your physical health,' she said.

The first step is learning to be kind to yourself, and the second is to try to reduce your stress so you can free up some more brainpower. Beating yourself up, or engaging in blaming and shaming, is not going to help. Nor is arguing with or blaming your partner or family. You'll also need to identify ways of reducing your stress that resonate with you – preferably those that don't involve taking the credit card for a walk.

The dopamine effect

What do you do when you are stressed? Do you eat chocolate? Have a gin and tonic? Go shopping? Smoke? One of the obvious things to do when going through financial hardship is to cut back on expenses. Most of the things I just listed hinge on items of discretionary spending. However, when we are stressed, we automatically seek what makes us feel better. This is largely because of the effect of dopamine.

Dopamine is a neurotransmitter made in the brain, and its release is what makes us feel happy. Basically, when our brains feel good, as if we're getting a reward, it's due to the release of dopamine. When we're stressed out, we're not experiencing that sweet dopamine effect, that happy feeling, and so our instinct is to do something to get it.

Our brains produce dopamine when we do or experience pleasurable things – love (or sex), great food or the smell of a brand-new car – and this is where those discretionary spending habits come in. Marketers know the effect that dopamine has on us, and we've been conditioned to use 'retail therapy' (or things such as drinking, overeating or even playing the pokies) to solve problems such as relationship breakdowns, career disappointments or bad news. And yes, I've bought new frocks to cheer myself up during relationship difficulties, or gone op-shopping for 'bling' or had too much to eat or drink when upset at work. We all do it, but it doesn't necessarily solve our problems. Sometimes it even makes them worse.

One way this can be a problem is if it becomes an addiction that contributes to financial stress. Another is that, despite being the last thing our wallets need, discretionary spending is often something we turn to when we suddenly land in financial stress. If this is something you identify with, it's important to find new ways to deal with and manage stress that don't require you to spend. If you address this, it's going to help with the next steps.

To move forward, confront the issue causing you financial difficulty and stress and then take action, it's important to develop a rewards system to celebrate the small wins as you go along. Maybe you put gold stars into your diary when you do certain positive things. Or maybe you go for a walk immediately after you do something stressful, such as opening an overdue notice that has arrived in the mail. Whatever it is, well done you!

If you're helping someone in financial difficulty, it's important to recognise and understand the emotional impact of what they're experiencing. You might feel frustrated that they don't just face the music and *do* something about their problem, and it can be tempting to charge in and take control. It's easy to be judgmental about spending habits such as smoking, drinking or gambling in the face of financial ruin, but it's so important to have empathy for what others are going through and understand why it's so difficult for them to make decisions while under that sort of pressure. They're probably in survival mode and resorting to unhelpful and expensive behaviours because of the dopamine effect. If it's you who's coping through behaviours that are making your financial hardship worse rather than better, remember that you're also worthy of this compassion and understanding. The more you beat yourself up about it, the more you resort to those behaviours.

Having the courage to acknowledge there is a problem

It's easy to act like an ostrich and stick your head in the sand pretending the problem doesn't exist. But problems don't just go away, and to paraphrase existentialist philosopher Jean-Paul Sartre, not choosing is still a choice. In my experience, problems only get worse until you do something about them. Once you understand how compound interest works, you can also see that interest will literally only make your loan repayments worse – on a daily basis – until you take action.

The first step is acknowledging there's a problem. That takes real courage, but it takes even more courage to do something about it. It's important to have a clear picture of your financial situation so you know what you're dealing with. This can be especially hard if you've been in denial for a while – and let's face it, it's hard to be super chipper when dealing with financial hardship.

You're going to need to work out things such as the number of debts you owe, repayments and when they are due, and the amount of income you have coming in to cover that (or not). You're also going to have to force yourself to look at bank and lender statements and open any letters lenders are sending you. Once you have a rough picture of what you owe and how much you have coming in, you'll need to create a budget. Making a budget will help you with the next step: requesting financial hardship assistance. It will also help you formulate a plan to repay – or determine that you can't. Yes, this is tough, but it's something you're going to have to do.

When April left her husband, she had no idea of the extent to which she was in debt. As high-flying IT consultants, they lived a good life. They drove luxury vehicles and went on overseas holidays. Because her husband ran their business, she never saw payslips and had no idea how much she really earned, and while she had an inkling all was not well, she didn't realise the extent until it was too late. April was so traumatised about the debt she was in that it was hard for her to do even simple things, such as look at bank statements. She found that she could only manage to focus on finances for ten minutes at a time. So that's what she did – she spent ten minutes a day managing her finances. April has now paid back all that debt, and she's now paying off the mortgage on her home with her new partner and two children.

Be proactive – ring your lender!

Are you ignoring emails from your lender? Throwing unopened letters into the bin? Are you worried about answering your mobile phone in case they call you? I once passed on a message from a bank to a colleague, not realising it was one of *those* phone calls. The atmosphere changed in seconds.

Yes, it's hard, but guess what? It won't be nearly as bad if you take the initiative and contact your lender. Just like ripping off a bandaid, sometimes it's easier to just get it over and done with.

We like to think that banks and other financial institutions are greedy and evil, trying to snaffle our property at bargain rates or rip us off. Yes, there are some shonky operators out there, especially in the payday loan area. However, most lenders are in the business of loaning money, not real estate. They don't want to repossess your home; that involves a lot of paperwork, expensive legal processes and *hassle*. Even if they successfully repossess a mortgagee's home and sell it, there's absolutely no guarantee that they would get back what they loaned – especially when they add up all the costs of the repossession process. Instead, most lenders want to keep you as their customer. Major banks have dedicated areas that specialise in working with people suffering from financial hardship. For instance, the Commonwealth Bank has a Financial Assistance Solutions team, and according to their website, they're 'here to help'.

I can imagine you're rolling your eyes and thinking, 'Yeah right – they're really going to help...' But while a lender is unlikely to go onto their computer and delete your mortgage (I wish!), they can often assist with a hardship variation (changes to help you manage short-term difficulties). This could include making it so that you don't have to make repayments (or that you pay a lesser amount) for a period of time, extend the loan term or convert your mortgage to interest-only repayments. Note that compound interest may mean it costs you more over the course of your loan if you do accept a hardship variation, but at the very least, they are less likely to hassle you with overdue loan notices.

When you talk to your lender's financial hardship team, make sure you're super polite. The person you'll speak to is a real person, just like you. They spend a large part of their day dealing with angry and upset people. If you are nice to them and communicate honestly and regularly about what is happening – and deliver on paying what you can afford – they are more likely to work with you to find a solution.

Extend your loan term

One way to stay afloat when experiencing short-term problems is to speak to your bank about extending the term of your loan. This will reduce your monthly repayments, which will put more cash in your pocket that can help you pay essential bills. Overall, this is cheaper than, say, relying on credit cards with interest rates of up to 24.99 per cent or, worse, payday lenders.

While extending the term of your loan can help you weather short-term storms, it's not a good long-term strategy. Pushing your mortgage term out means that the interest compounds over a longer period, and so you'll end up paying more interest.

For instance, say you have $600,000 owing on your mortgage on a 25-year term. To meet the terms, you'd be paying $3866 per month, and over the course of the loan you'd pay $559,743 in interest. If you were to extend it to 30 years (as shown in figure 6), you'd pay $269 less a month and, over the course of the loan, pay $695,029 in interest. But when times are tough, that $269 might make a huge difference.

Figure 6: Comparing monthly and total repayments for different terms

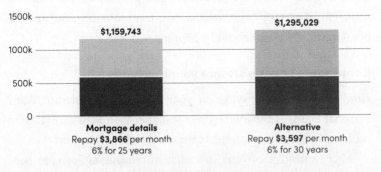

(SOURCE: MONEYSMART.GOV.AU)

If you do use this tactic, make sure that, once you get through your short-term shit, you make additional repayments to catch up.

Switch to an interest-only loan

Another option could be to switch to an interest-only loan. Interest-only loans are often favoured by property investors, especially those who are using a negative gearing strategy and chasing capital gain. Basically, they want to be able to claim investment 'losses', so they're not seeking to pay down the principal too quickly. It makes sense in that it's often a better strategy to focus on paying down your home loan rather than an investment loan.

However, overuse of interest-only loans, including for principal places of residence, was heavily criticised in the 2019 Royal Commission into Misconduct in the Banking, Superannuation and Financial Services Industry. Do you remember the example I gave in chapter 3 of the $1000 suit purchased on a credit card where only the minimum was repaid? It created a snowballing debt. The same thing happens with interest-only loans because you're not paying off any principal, just the interest on the debt.

As they enable you to continue to make lower repayments, using interest-only loans can be a good short-term solution – say, if you're going through a separation and plan to sell the property soon. However, they aren't healthy long-term solutions, and any use of interest-only loans should be handled with care.

Consolidate your debts into your mortgage

How much are you paying on your car loan? Credit card debt? Personal loans? If the interest rate is higher than your mortgage, it could make sense to consolidate these debts into your mortgage.

Many mortgage brokers specialise in refinancing loans to consolidate debt. It's a commonly used tactic that can help you achieve three things:

1. **Consolidate all debts into one easy payment.** Consolidating everything onto your mortgage makes it easier to track and repay. No more worrying about missing personal or car loan repayments.
2. **Pay less interest.** As the interest rate on your mortgage is generally lower than that of unsecured debt, you will be paying less interest if you consolidate that debt into your mortgage.
3. **Free up more cash to pay off your debt.** Because you will be paying less interest, you will have more cash to pay off your debts.

However, consolidating your debts into your mortgage is not a licence to spend. You still need to examine why you racked up these debts in the first place. Another often overlooked fact is that a mortgage is generally for a longer term than other personal debt.

Going back to that $1000 suit, you might be paying only 6 per cent interest rather than 24.99 per cent, but you'll be doing it over 30 years. That means that the compound interest snowball will build and build and build, and you could end up paying for your personal debt many times over.

Consolidating personal debt onto your mortgage can be a good strategy in the right circumstances, but it's important to make additional repayments to account for the longer term of the mortgage – and don't rack up new personal debt again.

The National Debt Helpline

Feeling a bit overwhelmed by all of this? The good news is that help is available. The National Debt Helpline (1800 007 007) is a free, not-for-profit service. The people on the other end of the phone line are trained financial counsellors, and their role involves a willingness to listen and not judge.

I had the privilege of chatting on my podcast with Nicole Flaws, a former counsellor from Care, which is part of the National Debt Helpline. According to Nicole, it's really hard for people to ask for help – and they often leave it until it's quite late.

'As a society, we're generally pretty helpful people,' she said. 'We're happy to help our friends, even strangers and family. But when it comes to *asking* for help, usually that's a really difficult thing. Particularly with finances, it can be [considered] a really shameful thing.'

Financial counsellors with the National Debt Helpline have seen it all – and the people who need help aren't always who you think. We tend to think that only 'poor' people struggle with money and debt, but people earning big incomes can also get into strife.

'People who might be on good salaries and think, well, I shouldn't be in this situation,' said Nicole. 'I'm not sure why I'm struggling here.

So, it is a deeply personal thing to be feeling financial hardship or feel you're not quite able to make these payments.'

According to Nicole, when someone calls a financial counsellor it's often the first time they've talked about their financial issues.

'It's a deeply personal thing, and a lot of people don't disclose it to their partners or their friends,' she said. 'They have picked up the phone, and they made the call. And usually, I try to reassure people that that's the hardest part of the process.'

Financial counsellors generally recommend that people contact them if they are feeling overwhelmed, uncomfortable or a bit unsure of what's happening. They recognise that financial problems can feel overwhelming, and they can work with you to do things such as develop a budget and negotiate to make small repayments on loans. They can often help you talk to your lenders to explain what is happening.

Do you or a friend feel you need to learn more about money and finances? Care has some useful free resources that you can access online. The National Debt Helpline also has resources you can use for dealing with mortgage problems specifically. These include tips for approaching your lender and accessing mortgage hardship repayment options.

Remember, if things have become really out of hand and you or a friend aren't coping, please reach out to organisations such as Lifeline (13 11 14) and Beyond Blue.

Make a complaint

Has your lender done something dodgy, such as levy incorrect fees or charges? Do you feel that you have been wronged? If so, you might want to consider making a complaint to AFCA, which is Australia's ombudsman for financial complaints. It describes itself as a non-government alternative to the courts, and its service is free.

AFCA can't consider all complaints for everything. You can't complain to them just because you can't make your repayments or because you borrowed too much, but you *can* complain to them if there's been a serious fault on behalf of your lender, such as them telling you things that weren't true in the application process. Though it can't wave a magic wand and make debts go away, AFCA can work with people experiencing financial hardship to find an outcome with their lender – and sometimes, to find a solution, you just need an advocate. You can also request ACFA's assistance if your lender refuses a hardship request.

Here is a broad overview of the process of working with AFCA to resolve a complaint:

1. Contact your lender. As I detailed earlier in this chapter, many lenders have dedicated teams, and they may be able to help you by reducing payment amounts, delaying payments or stopping them for a period of time.

2. If you're not happy with the outcome, you've asked for hardship relief and your lender has refused, or your lender commences legal proceedings, lodge a complaint with AFCA. You can do this online.

3. ACFA will work with you and your lender to reach an outcome. ACFA says that most complaints are resolved during this step.

4. If a solution cannot be found through negotiation, AFCA can make a final decision.

Ask for support from family and friends

It might seem like an obvious thing to do, but people are often reluctant to ask for support when money is involved. I don't mean asking family and friends for a loan – it can complicate those relationships – but there might be other ways they can help out, including offering emotional support. A problem shared is often a problem halved. By telling others that you're in financial difficulty, you're really facing up to the problem, and that's the first step to getting back on track.

Throughout this book I've shared tips and strategies to help you pay off your mortgage in 10 years, but they're equally applicable when you're facing difficult times. When shit happens, you'll need to really turbocharge everything you've learned to get through. This is when asking for help can be a game changer. For example, if you tell your parents about your difficulties, they may offer to mind the children for a short period of time to save on childcare fees. A friend may be looking for accommodation and offer to rent out your spare room for a short while. Another friend might need a hand on the weekend in their shop or cafe and offer you a short-term, part-time job. If no-one knows, no-one can help.

Summary

- If you or someone you know is dealing with financial problems, it's important to recognise that it's stressful – and that this stress may make it harder to think and act rationally to fix the problem.

- If you're spending too much money because you're stressed, it could be due to the dopamine effect. Developing a new, positive rewards system that doesn't involve spending is important as you deal with your debt issue.

- Be proactive: call your lender before they call you. Ignoring letters or phone calls won't make them go away, but communicating with your lender might.

- Your lender's hardship assistance program might include things such as extending your loan term or reducing repayments. Note that this doesn't make your mortgage disappear, but it can help as you find a solution to short-term problems.
- Consolidating personal debts onto your mortgage is a common strategy. It can be a good strategy as the other personal debt will be on an overall lower interest rate, but it's important to make additional mortgage repayments when you're back on track.
- Call the National Debt Helpline if a debt is leaving you or someone you know feeling overwhelmed or anxious. Their trained financial counsellors are there to help.
- If your lender has done something shonky or denies you hardship assistance, you can make a complaint to AFCA.

Sometimes shit happens, and that can make it hard to stay on top of your mortgage repayments – forget about getting ahead. What's important is that you acknowledge the problem and ask for help. When you're no longer under financial stress, you can get back to your goal.

Chapter 17

Congratulations!

Congratulations! You've paid off your mortgage. Now what?

Paying off your mortgage, no matter its size, is a huge achievement, and while you're focused on that it can be hard to think about the next steps. This chapter is designed to give you some ideas about how you might celebrate and how you might go about setting new financial goals.

Discharge your mortgage – or not

You might think that your lender will contact you or do something special to mark you reaching $0 on your mortgage. While you might pop a bottle of champagne to celebrate, they aren't likely to contact you at all. So, what happens next? Well, unless you reach out to them, nothing. Absolutely nothing. In fact, I know of an older couple who continued to use their mortgage as their savings account, amassing $80,000 in surplus. Initially, I was horrified because that's $80,000 that they could have been investing. But they weren't paying bank fees, and the return they might have been getting elsewhere at that time was minimal.

Keeping your mortgage open and using it as a savings account – as this couple did – is not ideal because you typically earn nothing on that money when you could have been investing it. However, there *is* a key advantage to keeping your mortgage open: you can use it as a line of credit. You might not think you need money, but the week after you pay off your mortgage your car might die and you might need a new one. Or you might suddenly decide to upgrade your house. Or there could be a family emergency. You might be surprised how often you need access to cash once your mortgage is paid off. Of course, you can get a personal loan, but that'll be at a higher rate. You could also refinance your mortgage to release equity, but that requires paperwork.

When I paid off my suburban home in 2016, I had vague plans to sell and move somewhere that would require less of a commute. At the time, I pondered whether to discharge the mortgage and invest excess cash coming in. I'm glad I didn't, because for various reasons I ended up buying a new place within months, and having access to the mortgage meant I had easy access to money for the deposit.

Still, no-one can deny that it's a great feeling to own your property unencumbered. When you're ready to kick your lender off your title, there are a few steps you'll need to follow.

The process

The first thing to do is contact your lender and ask about the discharge process. Usually this involves filling out a discharge authority form and paying the lender a fee. Yes, you'll have to pay a fee of anywhere between $50 and $600 to discharge your mortgage. But wait, there's more. Your lender will then need to prepare a discharge of mortgage document. They'll return that to you, and you'll then need to register it with your state or territory lands department.

(In the ACT, where I live, it's the ACT Land Titles Office.) When I did this a few years ago it was quick and easy, though it still required an in-person visit to a government shopfront. I had to fill out a discharge of mortgage form and pay an additional $160, but within minutes my property was mortgage free. Yah!

In the old days, after going through the process of discharging your mortgage, you would receive a piece of paper showing your unencumbered ownership, but this is mostly done electronically now. It's also relatively straightforward to search on a property to see if there are any caveats such as mortgages on it.

Set a new investment goal

Okay, you're mortgage free – hooray! Time to get out the margaritas, sit back and relax. No need to budget anymore. Now you can go spend, spend, spend. After all, you'll have several thousand extra dollars in cash every month that you no longer need to put onto your mortgage. Right?

Not so fast. You've achieved a significant goal, but it's easy to stagnate if you don't have a plan in mind. Trust me when I say that it's easy to leak money without a clear goal. So, the next step is to make one.

Often, the next goal revolves around investing – specifically, investing to achieve financial independence. One woman, who goes by Latestarterfire publicly, paid off the mortgage on her home and then lost interest in finance completely. She thought about buying an investment property but left it on the backburner and didn't do anything about it. Then at age 47 she realised that she was just wasting her money and, unless she wanted to continue to have to work full-time as a health care worker until she was much older, needed to do something about it. Latestarterfire is now a prolific blogger and Instagrammer who encourages and motivates people to achieve financial independence. She invests in her superannuation and on the share market (in particular in exchange traded funds, or ETFs), and she's able to work less and afford some amazing travel while tracking one year ahead of her goal to retire at 55.

What does financial freedom and success look like to you? Do you plan to take time off to travel or start a family? Do you want to join many in the Financial Independence, Retire Early (FIRE) movement and retire in your 30s or 40s? Or even in your 20s? Or do you want to keep working, amass investments and be wildly wealthy? The choice is yours, but it starts with setting a new financial goal and sticking to it. Having your mortgage paid off provides a rock of financial stability that you can use as a springboard for your next financial goal.

Prepare for emergencies

Assuming you were ahead of your mortgage payments before paying it off (which you would have been if you were implementing the steps in this book), you would most likely have been able to use your mortgage as an emergency fund. In other words, if there was a crisis and you needed money in a hurry, you could withdraw funds from your mortgage via your redraw facility.

As I mentioned at the start of this chapter, you will no longer have quick and easy access to these funds if you discharge your mortgage. You could still use your mortgage to store savings, but I don't recommend it as there are better ways to invest. While you may have other investments, such as shares, you might not want to be forced to liquidate those to pay for emergencies and essentials if a crisis hits you during a downturn. The issue, then, is finding a new way to save and hold money so that you're prepared for an emergency.

The first step is to work out how much money you need in an emergency fund. It's an individual preference, but as a rule of thumb I would suggest at least three months' worth of income and no more than 12. If you are risk-averse, you may wish to have more money than someone who feels confident they'll always find a solution to a problem. While the emergency fund is all about reducing risk, there's an opportunity cost in storing it conservatively rather than investing it.

Next, you need to figure out where you're going to invest your emergency fund. The emergency fund is more about security than large investment returns, so a bank account will often work best for parking your money. Your emergency fund is different to a normal savings account. You will (hopefully) only be depositing money, not withdrawing it – except in case of emergency, of course. A term deposit isn't useful here as you might need to access money quickly, and an everyday savings account also isn't ideal as it generally attracts lower interest rates.

Accordingly, a high-interest savings account – preferably with low or no fees – is usually what you want for your emergency fund. There are many high-interest accounts available, so make sure you check out what your existing bank offers and do some research using an online finance comparison site such as Canstar, Finder or InfoChoice.

How secure is the money in your bank?

The 2008 Global Financial Crisis and the fall of overseas financial institutions such as Lehman Brothers and Bear Stearns provoked concern here in Australia about the impact on the deposits of Australian investors. In response, the Australian Government enacted the Financial Claims Scheme (FCS) to ensure financial protection for consumers in the unlikely event of the failure of a bank, credit union, building society or general insurer. The FCS provides a government-backed safety net for deposits up to $250,000 made in authorised deposit-taking institutions. In other words, if your bank, credit union or building society is covered under the FCS, then your deposit is guaranteed by the government. To see if you're covered, visit the deposit checker page on the Australian Prudential Regulation Authority (APRA) website.

Turn your focus to superannuation

Remember in chapter 11 where I worked out that someone could amass over $1.2 million if they forewent a cup of coffee every morning and instead put the money into their super? The reasons that strategy is so successful are the magic of compound interest and the tax advantages of superannuation.

Note also that I wasn't comparing apples with apples: I based my calculations on a 42-year working life, whereas the term of a typical mortgage is 30 years. Also, you can only put a limited amount of money into your superannuation to gain these benefits. The annual concessional cap at the time of writing is $27,500 (but it goes up regularly), meaning that you and your employer can contribute up to $27,500 through salary sacrificing and the compulsory superannuation guarantee levy. This reduces your assessable income for taxation purposes. Once these concessional contributions are in your superannuation fund, they will be taxed at 15 per cent. You might wonder how 15 per cent tax is a good outcome. Well, it's much less than many people pay in income tax, and it's also much less than you may pay on capital gains tax as your investment grows. In other words, it's one of the most tax-effective strategies out there.

If you're earning a good income, superannuation is a good perk, and it's important to spend some time researching and comparing super schemes. Should you pay off your home or invest in superannuation? I personally believe the answer is both, especially seeing as the annual concessional cap means that you need to start early and be in the long game. You can play catch-up to some extent if you don't contribute the full amount of the annual concessional cap, but the benefits of compound interest still mean it's ideal to start early and contribute regularly.

Once you've paid off your mortgage, I would suggest the first thing to do is to investigate how much you're contributing to super and see if you can contribute more. Note that if you overpay, you could wind up paying more in tax and even be fined, so it's important to do your sums carefully and get good financial advice.

Budget for travel

In chapter 15 I discussed balancing travel and a mortgage. When you're mortgage free, chances are travel could be a priority.

Once we paid off our mortgage, we budgeted for travel a different way. The first thing we did was commit to putting $300 aside – in a separate account – every fortnight. The reason for the separate account was to make it clear that this money was for travel. Spending a weekend at the coast and decide to go out for fish and chips? If it's part of your holiday spending, you can pay for it with your holiday money. It's easy enough to keep separate, and it makes it much easier to budget.

The other advantage of keeping your travel fund separate is that you can choose an account with higher interest rates that's also suited to international travel. Not all bank accounts are great for travelling. Many charge fees on overseas transactions or ATM withdrawals. We use a bank account that you can access a variety of different foreign currencies with and that has no monthly account, transaction or ATM fees. We also hold a credit card with the same bank, so we can still pay for holidays on the credit card to get the included travel insurance and transfer between the accounts quickly and easily.

Helping others

Once you're in a good financial situation, you may wish to help other people. Many of our friends, for instance, are now helping their children get into the property market. With the high cost of property, many parents feel that they should do whatever they can to help their kids, grandkids or even godchildren.

Deciding whether or not to help others is your decision to make. I'm not going to tell you whether you should or shouldn't do it. However, I do want to point out some of the key risks. Anyone who has ever been on an aeroplane and watched a safety demonstration knows that the advice is for you to fit your own oxygen mask before you put one on anyone else. This goes against the first instinct of most parents, which is to put the mask on their children first, but the advice has been given deliberately: we need to look after ourselves *before* we're in a position to help anyone else.

We need to apply this to the question of helping others get into the property market. Do you want to extend yourself so much that you'll end up couch surfing with your kids? I posed this hypothetical question to a client recently, and her answer was an emphatic no! So, before you even feel obligated to help your kids or others in your family, make sure you look at your own financial situation to ensure that you have enough set aside to protect youself in case of emergency or retirement. Make sure you don't go into debt to help anyone else. Secondly, be wary of going on someone else's title. If the money is a gift, give it as a gift. On my podcast, personal finance guru Noel Whittaker talked about a situation he had encountered with a client who had helped a child purchase a property. While they weren't living in the property or paying the mortgage, as they had contributed to the deposit they registered their name on the title deed. The only problem was that, when it came time for them to retire, they weren't eligible for the pension, as on paper they had an investment property.

Summary

- Congratulations on reaching your goal of paying off your mortgage!

- If you do not discharge your mortgage and instead retain it, you might be able to redraw funds if there is an emergency.

- When it's time to discharge that mortgage, be aware that there will be a process to go through involving forms and fees.

- To avoid financial stagnation, it's a good idea to set a new investment goal to work towards once your mortgage is paid off.

- An emergency fund set up in a high-interest savings account can help cover you if you need money quickly for something unexpected.

- It's important to invest in superannuation as part of an overall investment strategy, but after paying off your mortgage it's a good idea to review and see if you could pay – and benefit – more.

- Post-mortgage, you may wish to travel more. One way to budget for this is to have funds in a separate account to isolate travel expenses and take advantage of certain account features suited to your travel ambitions.

While paying off your mortgage needs to be a priority for a while, it's worth thinking about what you're going to do once it's gone. It's important to form a clear post-mortgage financial plan and stick to it, or else it can be easy to get into spendy habits. That said, it's also important to do something fun to celebrate your milestone, whether it's cracking open a bottle of champagne, enjoying a nice dinner out or going on a holiday.

Owning my home outright is, for me, a dream come true. As a mother to two children, it gives me a strong sense of security to know that I'm not at risk of being thrown out by a landlord. It has also given me confidence to invest in other things, and to try other things such as spending more time writing and founding a startup. While I'm currently back in the workforce, I don't feel chained to a job, and I feel that this gives me more financial freedom. I can't wait for you to experience that as well.

Acknowledgements

Many thanks to you – the reader – for choosing to purchase this book. I hope it brings you much joy and abundance.

Thank you to Lesley Williams at Major Street Publshing, who persuaded me to write this book with haste in the spirit of imperfect action. Thank you also to Lauren Mitchell, who worked tirelessly to edit this book and ensure that all facts were correct and the tone was encouraging rather than negative.

A big thank you to my frugal mentor and friend Trish Smith for her help and inspiration. She's referred to many times in this book for good reason: she's awesome.

Thank you to the many people whose stories I have shared in this book. I'm constantly inspired by the many inspirational financial and frugalista tips I learn from others, and I thank everyone quoted in this book for allowing me to share their stories. I also wish to thank all the personal finance authors and influencers who have come before me, especially those in the FIRE community. It's such an inspiring and collaborative group of people who are committed to helping others achieve financial independence.

Last, but not least, I would like to thank my husband Neil for his support and encouragement – including reading drafts while on a cruise ship. It's not easy being married to a writer: anything you say can be used in writing. He's lost count of the number of times he's met someone who has read something I've written and remarked, 'I really feel like I know you, Neil!'

About the author

Serina Bird is a finance writer, podcaster and money coach who helps people save money and live more meaningful lives. She hosts the podcast *The Joyful Frugalista* and is the author of *The Joyful Frugalista* and *The Joyful Startup Guide*. She is a regular contributor to *Money* and encourages people to spend less and save more (with joy) on the path to financial empowerment. Serina is also the editor of *The Moore Street Journal*, an online platform that promotes business and startup success in the Canberra region, and the founder of the online sustainable marketplace The Joyful Fashionista.

Serina is passionate about helping people find joy through financial empowerment. She has been joyfully frugal since before the cost of living made it an imperative, and she loves sharing tips, recipes and hacks that help people save money and save the planet. Serina is the former face of 'Savvy Shopper', a weekly column that ran in *The Daily Telegraph* during the COVID lockdowns of 2020. She has also been featured in Australia and globally in publications including *The Toronto Star*, *The Daily Mail*, *Sydney Morning Herald*, *The Sun-Herald*, *Woman's Day*, *New Idea* and *That's Life!* She is a regular guest on ABC and other radio broadcasters, and has appeared on television programs including *Studio 10*, *TODAY EXTRA*, *Sunrise* and *Mum's at the Table*.

References

Chapter 1: On being mortgage free

M Beach, 'Seventies trailblazer Ita Buttrose blazes a new trail in her 70s', *The West Australian*, 14 May 2019. thewest.com.au/lifestyle/stm/seventies-trailblazer-ita-buttrose-blazes-a-new-trail-in-her-70s-ng-b881183736z

N Khadem, 'Boomers, Generation X or Millennials: Who has it worse when it comes to buying a home and paying it off?', *ABC News*, 6 February 2023. abc.net.au/news/2023-02-06/baby-boomers-generation-x-millennials-housing-interest-rate-rise/101929468

AE Navidad, 'Marshmallow test experiment and delayed gratification', *SimplyPsychology*, 1 May 2023. simplypsychology.org/marshmallow-test.html

N Sweeney, 'Women buyers move into the property market', *Australian Financial Review*, 8 March 2022. afr.com/property/residential/women-buyers-move-into-the-property-market-20220307-p5a2ce

K Ziwica, 'Without meaningful intervention, the number of older homeless women will double', *Women's Agenda*, 6 October 2022. womensagenda.com.au/latest/women-and-homelessness/

Chapter 2: Crunching the numbers

Australian Bureau of Statistics, 'Lending indicators', *ABS*, 5 May 2023. abs.gov.au/statistics/economy/finance/lending-indicators/latest-release

Australian Institute of Health and Welfare, 'Housing affordability', *AIHW*, 30 June 2021. aihw.gov.au/reports/australias-welfare/housing-affordability

InfoChoice, 'Compare home loan interest rates from 4.99%', *InfoChoice*, n.d. infochoice.com.au/home-loans/

J Kehoe, 'Lowe admits "embarrassing" error on 2024 rate rise', *Australian Financial Review*, 3 May 2022. afr.com/policy/economy/lowe-admits-embarrassing-error-on-2024-rate-rise-20220503-p5ai9e

N Khadem, 'Boomers, Generation X or Millennials: Who has it worse when it comes to buying a home and paying it off?', *ABC News*, 6 February 2023. abc.net.au/news/2023-02-06/baby-boomers-generation-x-millennials-housing-interest-rate-rise/101929468

N Khadem, 'RBA boss Philip Lowe says rate rises hurting households, indications are they will go higher', *ABC News*, 17 February 2023. abc.net.au/news/2023-02-17/inflation-interest-rate-rises-mortgage-stress-up-philip-lowe-rba/101988692

S Megginson, 'Compare home loan interest rates from 4.99%', *Finder*, finder.com.au/home-loans

Money, 'Compare home loans', *Money*, n.d. moneymag.com.au/compare/home-loans-mortgage-rates

J Sale & S Mickenbecker, 'Home loan comparison, *Canstar*, n.d. canstar.com.au/home-loans/

D Taylor, 'Australia's inflation problem is now entrenched and that means interest rates have to rise again', *The Drum*, 29 January 2023. abc.net.au/news/2023-01-29/australia-inflation-problem-entrenched-interest-rates-rise-again/101897468

Chapter 3: Compound interest and your mortgage

J Eyers, '$70,000 home loan "loyalty tax" netting banks $4.5b', *Australian Financial Review*, 1 August 2022. afr.com/companies/financial-services/70-000-home-loan-loyalty-tax-netting-banks-4-5b-20220729-p5b5m8

Chapter 4: Goal-setting and mindset strategies to reduce your mortgage

Australian Bureau of Statistics, 'Lending indicators', *ABS*, 5 May 2023. abs.gov.au/statistics/economy/finance/lending-indicators/latest-release

J Eyers, '$70,000 home loan "loyalty tax" netting banks $4.5b', *Australian Financial Review*, 1 August 2022. afr.com/companies/financial-services/70-000-home-loan-loyalty-tax-netting-banks-4-5b-20220729-p5b5m8

D Hughes, 'The 'cheap' mortgage refinance deals that cost borrowers more', *Australian Financial Review*, 24 March 2021. afr.com/companies/financial-services/the-cheap-mortgage-refinance-deals-that-cost-borrowers-more-20210322-p57cyd

S Megginson, 'Compare home loans with offset accounts', *Finder*, 9 January 2023. finder.com.au/offset-accounts

Moneysmart, 'Life insurance claims comparison tool', *moneysmart. gov.au*, n.d. moneysmart.gov.au/how-life-insurance-works/life-insurance-claims-comparison-tool

Chapter 5: Finance hacks for repaying your mortgage fast

T Harford, 'How the world's first accountants counted on cuneiform', BBC World Service, 12 June 2017. bbc.com/news/business-39870485

E DuBose, 'Does HECS-HELP debt affect your home loan borrowing power?', *Mozo*, 19 April 2023. mozo.com.au/home-loans/articles/does-hecs-debt-affect-borrowing-power

N Tovey, 'Get your credit score', *Canstar*, 25 May 2023. c anstar.com.au/credit-score/

Chapter 6: Insurance audit

J Blakkarly, 'Home owners drop unaffordable insurance as extreme weather risks grow', *Choice*, 24 August 2022. choice.com.au/money/insurance/home-and-contents/articles/home-insurance-climate-change

Defence Service Homes, 'Is your home at risk of underinsurance?', *Department of Veterans' Affairs*, 17 May 2021. dsh.gov.au/your-home-risk-underinsurance

D Graham, U Mihm & P Engel, 'How to avoid health insurance price hikes', *Choice*, 5 April 2023. choice.com.au/money/insurance/health/articles/how-to-avoid-health-insurance-premium-hikes

Medibank, 'Do I need health insurance if I'm turning 31?', *Medibank*, n.d. medibank.com.au/health-insurance/understanding-health-insurance/guides/turning-31/

National Road Safety Partnership Program, 'NRSPP Q&A: Road trauma and young drivers – does gender make a difference?', *NRSPP*, 2018. nrspp.org.au/resources/road-trauma-and-young-drivers-does-gender-make-a-difference/

A Richard & U Mihm, 'Save up to $935 by switching health insurance', *Choice*, 19 January 2022. choice.com.au/money/insurance/health/articles/health-insurance-hacks-that-will-save-you-money

K Sheppard, 'What are the cheapest cars to insure in 2022?', *Canstar*, 8 February 2022. canstar.com.au/car-insurance/cheapest-cars-to-insure/

Chapter 7: Waste not, want not

R Ciaramidaro, 'Which supermarket has the cheapest groceries?', *Choice*, 21 October 2021. choice.com.au/shopping/everyday-shopping/supermarkets/articles/cheapest-groceries-australia

United Nations Environment Programme, Food Waste Index Report 2021, *UNEP*, 4 March 2021. unep.org/resources/report/unep-food-waste-index-report-2021

Chapter 8: Taking out Takeaway

Australian Bureau of Statistics, 'Retail Trade, Australia', *ABS*, 3 May 2023. abs.gov.au/statistics/industry/retail-and-wholesale-trade/retail-trade-australia/latest-release

D Heckscher, 'What's the average spend on food delivery apps?', *Canstar*, 11 May 2023. canstarblue.com.au/stores-services/average-food-delivery-cost/

T Moore, 'Uber Eats Statistics', *MoneyAustralia*, 6 October 2022. moneyaustralia.net/uber-eats-statistics/

OzHarvest, 'Food waste facts', *OzHarvest*, n.d. ozharvest.org/food-waste-facts/

Chapter 9: Transport rethink

Australian Bureau of Statistics, 'Transport: Census', *ABS*, 28 June 2022. abs.gov.au/statistics/industry/tourism-and-transport/transport-census/latest-release

P Zaluzny & S O'Keefe, 'The best apps for finding cheap fuel', *Choice*, 29 September 2022. choice.com.au/transport/cars/general/articles/cheap-fuel-apps-review?

Chapter 10: Subscriptions sneak up on you

H Achauer, 'Why Are We All Still Watching TV Right Before Bed?', *Sleep Foundation*, 8 July 2022. sleepfoundation.org/sleep-news/watching-tv-before-sleep-most-popular-bedtime-routine

Australian Institute of Health and Welfare, 'Overweight and obesity', *AIHW*, 19 May 2023. aihw.gov.au/reports/australias-health/overweight-and-obesity

Australian Institute of Health and Welfare, 'Sleep problems as a risk factor for chronic conditions', *AIHW*, 26 November 2021. aihw.gov.au/reports/risk-factors/sleep-problems-as-a-risk-factor/summary

M Gabaji & C Stead, 'Foxtel vs Kayo: Which live streaming option is best for sports fans?', *Finder*, 19 April 2023. finder.com.au/kayo-vs-foxtel

D Heckscher, 'F45 Gyms Review & Guide', *Canstar*, n.d. canstarblue.com.au/stores-services/brands/f45-gyms/

A Lloyd, 'Financial treadmill: Aussies wasting $2.4 billion on unused gym memberships', *Finder*, 12 January 2021. finder.com.au/unused-gym-memberships

A Meade, 'Australian households spend $4,500 a year on entertainment, with streaming and gaming taking biggest slice, report says', *Guardian*, 20 July 2022. theguardian.com/media/2022/jul/20/australian-households-spend-4500-a-year-on-entertainment-with-streaming-and-gaming-taking-biggest-slice-report-says

Mens Health Staff, 'Couples with this piece of decor in their room have less sex', *Australian Men's Health*, 1 May 2021. menshealth.com.au/couples-with-tvs-in-the-room-have-less-sex/

PricewaterhouseCoopers, *Australian Entertainment & Media Outlook 2022–2026*, PwC, 2022. pwc.com.au/industry/entertainment-and-media-trends-analysis/outlook.html

Staff writers, 'Trendy gym, Cremorne Club, goes bust as $430 memberships voided', *news.com.au*, 21 April 2023. news.com.au/finance/business/other-industries/trendy-gym-cremorne-club-goes-bust-as-430-memberships-voided/news-story/4ce96ef70958325ce11e5 3a96d6c14a2

Chapter 11: The million–dollar coffee habit

Australian Associated Press, 'Australia the second thirstiest country for bottled water despite paying the highest prices, says UN report', *Guardian*, 17 March 2023. theguardian.com/australia-news/2023/mar/17/australia-the-second-thirstiest-country-for-bottled-water-despite-paying-the-highest-prices

E Fierberg, 'Suze Orman: How your daily coffee habit is costing you $1 million', *CNBC make it*, 28 March 2019. cnbc.com/video/2019/03/28/suze-orman-how-your-daily-coffee-habit-is-costing-you-1-million.html

K MacDonnell, '18 Australia Coffee Statistics in 2023: Interesting Facts!', *Coffee Addiction*, 4 January 2023. coffeeaffection.com/australia-coffee-statistics/

J Price, 'How to save on coffee as prices reach new high', *A Current Affair*, 2022. 9now.nine.com.au/a-current-affair/saving-on-coffee-as-prices-reach-new-high/76b9d2fb-a086-43fd-a03a-31dd13eb67b7

Sustainability Victoria, 'Eco-friendly alternatives to plastic water bottles', *SV*, 15 March 2023. sustainability.vic.gov.au/recycling-and-reducing-waste/at-home/avoid-waste/minimise-single-use-items/plastic-water-bottles

Chapter 12: Frugalista cleaning hacks

G Hing, 'Aussies spending $4b on cleaning services to tidy up this spring', *The Daily Telegraph*, 7 October 2018. dailytelegraph.com.au/news/nsw/aussies-spending-4-billion-cleaning-services-to-tidy-up-this-spring/news-story/60d987848cb3586f0275c8f25ea9f377

K Ho, 'Over a third of Aussies have bought more home cleaning products since pandemic', *YouGov*, 14 April 2021. au.yougov.com/news/2021/04/14/over-third-aussies-have-bought-more-home-cleaning-/

Chapter 13: Make some extra money for your mortgage

9News Staff, 'Gumtree's second hand economy booms to $46 billion during COVID-19', *9News*, 26 August 2020. 9news.com.au/national/coronavirus-australia-second-hand-economy-booms-46-billion/40c314b6-2c09-445e-8a4b-5c3c0285dc74

Animal Medicines Australia, 'Pets in Australia: A national survey of pets and people', *AMA*, 16 November 2022. animalmedicinesaustralia.org.au/report/pets-in-australia-a-national-survey-of-pets-and-people-2/ The Social Deck, 'Michael and Robert – founders of Parkhound', *Ideas Hoist*, 25 June 2015. ideashoist.com.au/michael-and-robert-founders-of-parkhound/

H Dervisevic, 'How much extra cash you can earn as an Airbnb host', *Savings.com.au*, 17 November 2022. savings.com.au/news/how-much-cash-you-earn-airbnb-host

D Morris, 'Hate Parking? Parkhound Connects You to Vacant Sydney Garages, Driveways and Car Parks Near You', *Broadsheet*, 9 November 2021. broadsheet.com.au/sydney/city-file/article/hate-parking-parkhound-connects-vacant-sydney-garages-driveways-car-parks-near-you

Chapter 15: Bring me a break

Australian Financial Complaints Authority, 'Credit, finance and loan products and issues', *AFCA*, n.d. afca.org.au/make-a-complaint/

credit-finance-and-loan-complaints/credit-finance-and-loan-products-and-issues

CommBank, 'Financial hardship', *CommBank*, n.d. commbank.com.au/support/financial-support/financial-hardship.html

A Mahdawi, 'Airbnb feels like staying with a cheap, uptight friend – then paying for the privilege', *Guardian*, 18 January 2023. theguardian.com/commentisfree/2023/jan/17/airbnb-feels-like-staying-with-a-cheap-uptight-friend-then-paying-for-the-privilege

Chapter 16: When shit happens

The Associated Press, 'Financial stress can induce drop in IQ', *CBC*, 3 September 2013. cbc.ca/news/science/financial-stress-can-induce-drop-in-iq-1.1326370

Australian Financial Complaints Authority, 'Financial hardship complaints', *AFCA*, n.d. afca.org.au/make-a-complaint/financial-difficulty

Australian Prudential Regulation Authority, 'About the Financial Claims Scheme', *APRA*, n.d. apra.gov.au/about-financial-claims-scheme

id. 'Deposit checker – Are your deposits protected?', *APRA*, n.d. apra.gov.au/deposit-checker-are-your-deposits-protected

Moneysmart, 'Hardship variation', *moneysmart.gov.au*, n.d. moneysmart.gov.au/glossary/hardship-variation

Care, 'Resources', *Care*, n.d. carefcs.org/resources

Financial Counselling Australia, 'Home loans', *National Debt Helpline*, n.d. ndh.org.au/Debt-problems/Home-loans/

Australian Financial Complaints Authority, 'Make a complaint', *AFCA*, n.d. afca.org.au/complain

Chapter 17: Congratulations!

Australian Prudential Regulation Authority, 'Deposit checker – Are your deposits protected?', *APRA*, n.d. apra.gov.au/deposit-checker-are-your-deposits-protected